THE COURAGE TO HOPE

THE COURAGE TO HOPE

by

Peter L Sampson

Scripture Union

130 City Road, London EC1V 2NJ

First published 1987

ISBN 0 86201 330 5

Phototypeset by Input Typesetting Ltd, London

Printed and bound in Great Britain
by Cox and Wyman Ltd, Reading

To the memory of John,
who taught me so much
in life and in death

CONTENTS

ACKNOWLEDGMENTS

I am grateful to the many people who have contributed towards the writing of this book. My thanks are especially due to Mary Parish, Evangeline Creighton and Jim Gatheral who read, corrected and commented on the manuscript. Their encouragement, together with that of my wife Kathleen and children Jayne and Jonathan, has enabled me to complete the work. I wish to thank Ruth Manson whose honest sharing from personal experience gave me insights into the loss of a child. Thanks also to Godfrey Rush for permission to use his poem 'Teddy Bears'. I am grateful to May MacDonald for typing my sabbatical notes and to my sister Joy Taylor who has typed and retyped the manuscript.

I am especially grateful to John's wife and family who gave me the privilege of walking some of the valley road with John. Finally my thanks are due to the many friends, especially in Chelmsford and East Kilbride, who in sharing their sorrows and hopes with me have enriched my life and furthered my ministry.

FOREWORD

Dying, death and grieving have for too long been taboo subjects. They are conversation-stoppers in most circles for many reasons – not least because of the fear of the unknown. It is the world of comedy that occasionally tries to break the silence, though without dispelling the mystery and uncertainty. Woody Allen's one-liner, 'It's not that I'm afraid to die. I just don't want to be there when it happens', highlights human nervousness at the prospect of dying.

Peter Sampson's book goes a long way in brushing aside the cobwebs of doubt and anxiety in the face of our mortality. He does not need to laugh at death in order to cope with it for he can bring to his subject the 'living hope' which has been given 'through the resurrection of Jesus Christ from the dead' (1 Peter 1:3).

This hope is not presented with any 'easy-believism' or attempt to sidestep the day-to-day realities of coping with terminal illness, watching a loved one die or grieving for that same person in the aftermath of death. For Peter Sampson is not only a caring and experienced pastor but has himself walked the road of witnessing the untimely dying of someone close.

John, Peter's friend of many years' standing, was to die of cancer over nine months – described as a 'nine month adventure' marked by 'a few, exhilarating peaks' and 'many dark valleys'. This excellent book took root in the ups and downs of that experience and was given further impetus by a three months' sabbatical, during which he worked for a while at St. Christopher's Hospice in London, as well as studying in depth the pastoral care of the dying and bereaved.

The result is a delightfully honest and loving exploration of the *normality* of facing death and grief. The writing is a healthy mix of Christian reflection and practical realism. Peter Sampson wrestles with the agonising dilemma of healing and continued suffering, tackles squarely the issues of pain control and the place of the Hospice Movement and deals sensitively with the practicalities of a loved one's last hours, the actual death, the funeral service and the stages of bereavement.

When Peter first knew that John had cancer he wrote down the words: 'To the glory of God – somehow'. This compelling book gives the 'somehow' of that glory on the path, trodden by both carer and cared for, through the shadowlands of dying and grieving. The perspective of Christian hope is that of the psalmist: 'Weeping may remain for a night, but rejoicing comes in the morning' (Psalm 30:5).

ROGER F HURDING

Introduction

It was a Wednesday afternoon in January. The telephone rang in my study. 'Hello, Peter, it's . . .' Why this telephone call from Essex to Scotland? I did not have to wait long for the reason. That morning John had received surgery, and a large malignant growth had been removed. His wife was phoning to give me the news. How much is concealed within that ominous word 'malignant' – uncertainty, fear, pain, suffering. Hope wavered.

So began a nine-month adventure, with a few exhilarating peaks, and many dark valleys. It was an adventure supremely for John, his wife and family, but shared in part by many friends of whom I was privileged to be one.

The friendship with John (the name is used to preserve anonymity) began sixteen years previously when I arrived fresh from theological college to become pastor in the Baptist church in Essex where John was a deacon. Being of a similar age and similar backgrounds, we became friends. We were able to bounce ideas off each other without fear of being misunderstood. In spite of my move to Scotland nine years later, the friendship deepened.

During the last nine months of John's life we kept in regular contact and had two family holidays together. I was privileged to spend the last ten days of his life with him.

A few months after his death I began a three month sabbatical, taking as my subject, 'The pastoral care of the dying and the bereaved.' In the Christian ministry I had experienced a sense of inadequacy and fear in the face of death and bereavement. Death was one of those subjects to hurry past. I found the grief of other people embarrassing. Death and bereavement had been outside my personal experience until John's death.

Following the telephone call about John's operation, I wrote down these words:

'To the glory of God – somehow.'

My faith was struggling to find hope.

At the time of John's illness and since his death, questions have flooded into my mind. So many questions! How should you pray for healing? How honest can you be with someone who is dying? What does it feel like to know that you do not have long to live? Can dying take place with faith and dignity? How do you cope with life after someone you love has died? How long does grief last? Supposing you feel angry with God, what do you do? These are some of the questions I have tried to answer in this book, for they are the questions asked by those struggling to hope in the face of death, dying and bereavement.

Do you know something of that struggle? Those who are seriously ill know it, and so do those who are caring for them. The carers may be family, friends, pastors or members of one of the caring professions. Those facing bereavement know the struggle, as do their friends who, at times, are at a loss to know how to bring comfort.

If you are wrestling with the spiritual and practical issues of death and bereavement, or are seeking to help one who is involved in this struggle, I pray that this book will be used to bring you God's courage to hope.

1
Divine healing

When John learnt that he had cancer it was not long before the question of healing was raised. We had often discussed the healing miracles of Jesus and the healings in the Acts of the Apostles. We had debated, and on one occasion acted upon, the teaching in James 5:14,15. We had read many books on the subject and listened to testimonies of healing. It had been a fascinating, heart-searching, though somewhat academic, experience. Now it was painfully personal. John was dying. The issue of divine healing was urgently practical. Healing mattered now as never before.

God does heal today

God is constantly at work, healing people in body, mind and spirit. He is still God our healer (Exod 15:26). However, his healing work is not necessarily miraculous, as Dr Roger Hurding points out in his book *As Trees Walking*.[1]

God's healing activity is through natural, medical and miraculous means. Sometimes the human body, created by God, heals naturally. At other times drugs and medicines are required. This medication is developed by scientists using God-given gifts, and raw materials from God's earth. At times God intervenes directly in the course of nature and performs a miracle.

Dr Hurding comments that God should be glorified in all three aspects of healing: healing by miracle is not more divine than healing by natural or medical means. An openness to divine healing must include an openness to whatever means God chooses. He works within and beyond the world of medicine.

The prayer of faith

The New Testament speaks of the prayer of faith being offered by the leaders of the church at the invitation of someone who is ill:

> Is any one of you sick? He should call the elders of the church to pray over him and anoint him with oil in the name of the Lord. And the prayer offered in faith will make the sick person well; the Lord will raise him up. If he has sinned, he will be forgiven. Therefore confess your sins to each other and pray for each other so that you may be healed. The prayer of a righteous man is powerful and effective.
> (Jas 5:14–16)

To anyone searching for the principles behind divine healing, a careful study of this passage will be rewarding. Here is a clear promise about the healing ministry of God – 'the Lord will raise him up . . . 'This ministry is firmly set within the context of the local church, and involves its spiritual leadership. Healing from God is channelled through believing prayer. The link – a direct one in some instances – is established between suffering and sin, healing and forgiveness. It is the Lord, not the prayer of faith, who raises up the sick man. The human channels that God may choose to use must be clean, for 'The prayer of a *righteous* man is powerful and effective.' These are but a few of the principles behind divine healing.

Does this passage indicate that if the conditions are carefully met God will always, must always, heal? That depends on whether it is the will of God for all sickness in his children to be healed in this life. There are several indications in the New Testament that God's will for us in this life includes healing only sometimes.

Jesus did not heal every sick person he met. At the pool of Bethesda there lay a large and pitiful number of blind, lame and paralysed people. Jesus chose one person for healing, a man who had been an invalid for thirty-eight years. Furthermore, the reason for only one person being healed seemed to lie within the sovereign will of God, and not within the faith, or lack of it, of the people. Why did Jesus heal only one among many? We do not know.

In the early church not every illness was healed. Paul advised Timothy, 'Stop drinking only water, and use a little wine because of your stomach and your frequent illnesses' (1 Tim 5:23). For Timothy the medicinal use of wine, rather than the miraculous intervention of the divine, was the way forward in time of illness. The sickness of Trophimus (2 Tim 4:20) and God's dealing with Paul's 'thorn in the flesh' (2 Cor 12:7–10) are further pointers towards the conclusion that it was not always God's will to heal his children. To assume that no Christian should remain ill, or that more faith and more prayer will bring healing, are assumptions lacking solid biblical foundation.

It would be dangerous, therefore, to conclude that the promise in James about God raising the sick man can be claimed *every* time one of his children is ill. It may not be God's will to heal in a particular instance. Scripture and experience tell us that God heals some and not others. Whether God will heal, and when and how he may heal, are questions that lie within his sovereign, and often mysterious, will. A biblical approach to healing must always recognize that God's thoughts and ways are higher than ours (Isa 55:8,9).

These marvellous verses in the book of James shed a powerful beam on the subject of divine healing, but it is only a beam lighting a part, not a floodlight illuminating the whole.

How crucial is faith?

Jesus often searched for some evidence of faith before he healed someone. After the healing he likewise acknowledged the presence of faith. To the woman in the crowd who touched the hem of his cloak, he said, 'Daughter, your faith has healed you' (Mark 5:34).

The faith that Jesus recognized was not necessarily found in the person who was healed: it was the centurion's servant who was healed, but his master's faith that drew a comment from Jesus (Luke 7:1–10). Faith certainly has a place within divine healing, but maybe a smaller one than is sometimes thought.

Have you ever been bewildered by God's choice of whom he heals, and even more, of those he does not heal? Dr Ruth Kopp frankly admits that those whom God heals are not often the ones she would 'nominate for healing on the basis of faith, prominence in Christian work, or purity of life'.[2] Sometimes God heals those whose faith seems to us to be nominal, and he refuses healing to a Christian with a tenacious faith. Faith, though it has a place, is not the most crucial issue in divine healing. God's sovereign will is the all-important factor.

What do we pray for?

A group of leaders in my first pastorate met to pray for the wife of one of them who was seriously ill with cancer. Some prayed simply and specifically that the Lord would heal Ann. Others prayed with the same fervour that God's will, whatever it was, would be accomplished. Thus two groups emerged, and a tension between them was felt. Were the two requests contradictory and a denial of our unity in the Spirit? Was one group more in touch with God than the other? Did one group have more faith than the other? The tension was painful.

Some answers to these questions came a few days later from the third chapter of the book of Daniel. Shadrach, Meshach and Abednego were about to be hurled into the blazing furnace by King Nebuchadnezzar. They expressed their faith, both in God's power to deliver them and in his right to choose whether to deliver them:

> If we are thrown into the blazing furnace, the God we serve is able to save us from it, and he will rescue us from your hand, O king. But even if he does not, we want you to know, O king, that we will not serve your gods . . .
> (Dan 3:17,18)

The words 'if he does not' are an example of faith holding to the sovereign control of God in human life; they are not an example of faith faltering. Shadrach, Meshach and Abednego expressed certainty about the *ability* of God to deliver them. Praying in faith does not require a detailed knowledge of God's will, but rather a knowledge of his nature as sovereign. The person who prays, 'Lord heal' does not have a greater faith than the person who prays, 'Thy will be done.'

Can I pray for healing?

For weeks John wrestled with the question, 'Can I pray for healing for myself?' Much heart-searching took place. Past experiences warned him about wrong emphases on faith. He knew that faith was ultimately a gift from God, not an attitude we manufacture ourselves. He also knew that we cannot use faith to manipulate God; faith cannot twist God's arm. Neither can faith demand healing from God by the careful selection of biblical verses. In fact faith cannot demand, it can only request.

John had always acknowledged the seriousness of his illness. He had asked frank questions and received honest answers about the cancer. He knew that, but for an intervention by God, he was going to die. Courageously, he faced the reality of the situation by tidying his business affairs and making provision for his family's future. Praying for healing was not to be some kind of game he played while deep down he was not prepared to face facts. John faced the fact that he might die, before he prayed for healing.

Neither was the prayer of faith to be a denial of the great hope of heaven. Joseph Bayly issued a timely warning: if the prayer of faith 'obscures the reality of heaven and its joyful prospect for the person who is ill . . . it is less than Christian'. The mere prolonging of life on earth is the vain hope of the unbeliever, while heaven is the goal of the believer. We should be wary lest the prayer of faith makes death appear as 'faith's defeat instead of heaven's door'.[3]

John's struggle to sort out motives continued. He was troubled. Was he being selfish in requesting healing for himself? Such a request must be for God's glory and not selfish ends. Thus a strong desire for God to be honoured filled John's mind at this time.

Yet another obstacle blocked his prayer for healing. Such a specific prayer was contrary to the way he had prayed in the past. In prayer meetings when some prayed with boldness for healing, John prayed cautiously. In his mind, praying for healing was associated with presumption and immaturity. How could he pray for healing, especially his own, after all he had said, taught and prayed in the past? God showed him that this hesitation was the grotesque sin of pride, masquerading as spiritual maturity, or, to use one of Dr William Sangster's expressions, 'pride wearing a halo'. Pride would not permit John to do what in the past had made him suspicious and critical. Only after he had been humbled by God, and confessed the sin of pride, could John answer 'Yes' to the question, 'Can I pray for healing for myself?'

'Sovereign Lord . . . Thy will be done'

When you pray for healing, lurking in the back of your mind may be the thought, 'Supposing God says "No", what then?' Some people will push that question hurriedly out of their heads, scolding themselves for their lack of faith. For John such a manoeuvre would not have been an act of faith but an act of dishonesty. So the possibility of handling a divine refusal had to be faced, not buried under so-called faith. Again John saw that it was pride that caused him to hesitate praying for healing, in case God said 'No'. Pride cannot cope with God's refusals, humility can.

The humility of Jesus in the garden of Gethsemane was given to John. As Jesus prayed 'not my will, but yours be done' (Luke 22:42), in similar fashion John prayed for healing. Together with two friends, the simple prayer was offered. Healing from God was requested, and the answer was left in God's hands. It was not a closed prayer that made demands on God. It was a prayer that began 'Sovereign Lord' and ended 'Thy will be done'. It was a prayer expressing belief in God's power to heal, and humble submission to his will.

One simple truth became so real at this time. We saw that it was all right for us as God's children to ask our heavenly Father for healing. It was not wrong for us to share with God what was on our hearts. The request for healing was just that, a request not a demand. Furthermore, it was a prayer that God would be glorified as the power of Jesus Christ was displayed.

A plea for balance

John struggled to come to the position where he could pray for his own healing. But he did arrive there, pray for healing, and receive God's peace. It was then very important to leave the matter of healing in God's hands. In time it became obvious that God was not healing, but was preparing John to leave this life for the fuller life in heaven. A preoccupation with divine healing would, at this point, have hindered God's gentle leading of John to an acceptance of death as being the next event in life.

James Casson, in his remarkable little book *Dying – The Greatest Adventure of My Life*, tells of the conflict he knew when his thoughts were centred on healing. Peace of mind came only when the issue of healing was left in God's sovereign hands. He writes of the release that . . .

> came with the realisation that the whole issue was out of my hands. One morning I had a clear picture that I was in a boat. Before, when asking for healing, it was as though I was in a punt where one stands at one end pushing at the punt pole and steering with more or less expertise. Afterwards, I was in a rowing boat, my back to the direction I was going, but travelling in a much more leisurely fashion. The great joy was that the Lord was at the tiller, his face gently smiling and his eyes twinkling as he quietly guided me to my destination.[4]

An overemphasis on healing, as well as hindering God's preparation for death, can also damage fellowship at a time when it is most necessary. If friends are constantly looking for healing, it becomes embarrassing to tell them that things are getting worse. So sustained fellowship is strained.

Sadly, the dying person may become isolated from his friends who are tenaciously holding on to the hope of healing, while the Lord is leading him along the valley of the shadow of death. Along this road are some very special blessings from the Shepherd who accompanies his sheep. There is a danger of forfeiting those blessings by wishing we were on another road. Let there be an emphasis on divine healing, but let it be balanced.

'There was something different . . .'

To the specific request for healing, God said 'No'. John was not healed of cancer in this life. But the prayer that God should be glorified and the power of Jesus Christ displayed *was* answered. Christ's power was seen in the healing of deep-seated pride. Christ's presence was seen in John throughout the intense suffering of his last weeks. The comment a nurse made to me a few minutes after John died assured me that God had been glorified: 'There was something different about your friend.' There was indeed – Jesus Christ.

2
To tell or not to tell?

'If you were dying, would you want to be told?' This blunt question was posed to a group of Christians of all ages. The majority indicated that they would want to be told. It is, of course, much easier to theorize on this question when you are enjoying sparkling health than to face it when you are weak and in pain. Nevertheless, surveys carried out among patients suffering from cancer have revealed a strong desire to know the truth.[1]

'I want to talk to you about my funeral arrangements,' said Mrs Bailey, in a business-like tone. This elderly lady, in her eighties, was lying on a hospital bed following a fall from which she had sustained a factured pelvis. Pneumonia had set in. She was dying and she knew it. With the courage and honesty characteristic of her life, she faced her death. My reaction, as her pastor, was less than honest: 'Now, Mrs Bailey, you are going to get better. You'll be surprised what they can do in this hospital.'

This incident, early in my ministry, gave me insights that have been confirmed many times. First, I learnt that the dying very often know that they are dying. They frequently know before they are told. With the terminally ill, 'telling them' is less an imparting of information and more a confirmation of something they already know. 'Telling them' is nevertheless still important, for it is the means by which a relationship of honesty is established. Second, I learnt how hard it is for family and friends to be honest with a dying person. Mrs Bailey wanted to be honest with me; I preferred to play games with her. I was grateful to a senior minister who urged me, on my next visit, to go along with Mrs Bailey's request to speak of her funeral.

Dishonesty hurts

When I refused to let Mrs Bailey speak of her death, I unwittingly increased her loneliness. The hospital staff were urging her to concentrate on getting well, even though they knew she was dying. I added to the isolation of that lady by saying things we both knew were untrue. Playing games with the dying is cruel: 'the truth from which the patient is being protected is the truth with which he is being forced to live in isolation'.[2] Furthermore, we rarely get away with lying to the dying, who seem to know instinctively when the truth is being covered up or only partly revealed.

We should remember that our silences, as well as our words, can tell lies. Dame Cicely Saunders quotes a patient who said, 'When the hospital said nothing, and my doctor said nothing, then I knew.'[3] Our silences can be frighteningly eloquent.

To be dishonest with a dying person can be degrading for him; it is to treat him as less than a person. We decide how to live and we have the right to decide how to die. It is when we take away from a person the ability to make decisions that we devalue that person. Dame Cicely Saunders tells of a patient who watched another patient die, clinging to a false hope of recovery. The observing patient commented, 'I can face dying, I can face pain, but what I can't face is being treated as less than a person.'[4] People have the right to live out their last days on something more than false hope.

Not only can dishonesty with the dying hurt them, it is wrong. So thinks Dr Ruth Kopp, who warns against the danger of 'playing God' when protecting the dying from the truth: 'To attempt to order the lives of others is to usurp the prerogative of God. And, while we are often unhappy with the way He orders His universe, most of us, in the last analysis, wouldn't really want His job!'[5]

Honesty breeds trust

Strong relationships are built on trust. To lie to a dying person is to undermine trust and to embark on a relationship that becomes increasingly unreal and irrelevant. When the advancing weakness in a patient's body and the hollow hopes expressed by visitors do not square, the patient will feel not only alone, but betrayed by those closest to him. When there is honesty about the approach of death, relationships are strengthened, love is deepened, prayer becomes relevant and God can speak from his word. I could only minister relevantly to Mrs Bailey when the two of us talked openly about death; then I knew how to pray with her and what scriptures to share. Honesty opens the door to effective ministry.

Honesty faces reality

To shield someone from the knowledge that he is dying could also lead to shielding him from a full experience of the goodness and sufficiency of God. For, in his need, the dying person may turn to the Lord in a unique way, and in the depth of that need discover the greater depth of God's grace.

From the outset of the Christian life, God requires us to be honest. Before discovering forgiveness, we learn that God desires 'truth in the inner parts' (Ps 51:6). Every subsequent step of spiritual growth requires the same painful facing up to ourselves or some challenge. Christianity is essentially a faith that faces reality and not one that provides escapist experiences. 'Face facts!' is the challenge of the living Christ throughout our lives. So in death the Christian is called to face the truth with Christ. When we do this we discover that the Christ who has supplied all our needs in life has infinite resources of grace to enable us to face death and dying. With Christ we need never fear being honest. We are told that all our needs will be met by God 'according to his glorious riches in Christ Jesus' (Phil 4:19). There are no exceptions to 'all your needs': death and dying are included in that phrase.

Honesty is fruitful

People can be happier knowing the truth. This was John's experience. Following abdominal surgery he was told that a large malignant growth had been removed. This information was given by the surgeon at John's request. During the remaining ten months of his life John spent much time preparing his family's future. With his wife he discussed the future of their three children. He retired from work and set in motion the complex process of selling his business. Matters relating to the house and finance were carefully investigated. With astonishing courage and vigour John made every possible provision for his family's future. Honesty had opened the door to loving service. Because he was willing to face the truth he continued to be a faithful husband and father to the end.

His honesty also did much to prepare his family and close friends for the long road of bereavement. He allowed the bereavement experience to begin before his death.

No time limit, please!

John made it clear to the surgeon that, while he wanted to know the result of the operation, he did not want to be given a time limit. Diagnosis, yes; prognosis, no. John felt it was both impossible and unnecessary to know how long he might have to live. He believed the question of timing should be left in God's hands.

Some people, on the other hand, do want to know how much time they have left. On this question we should proceed with extreme caution. Doctors are not omniscient and can rarely foretell the time of death with any accuracy, unless it is very close. Elisabeth Kübler-Ross is dogmatic on this issue of not giving a time limit: 'I think it is the worst possible management of any patient, no matter how strong, to give him a concrete number of months or years.'[6]

'He couldn't take it'

Families often try to protect a loved one from the truth of terminal illness, on the grounds that the patient could not handle the knowledge. 'He would crack', 'It would kill her.' Such statements are made to justify silence or 'white' lies. However, it is a fact that people can face the truth better than uncertainty. Ignorance and uncertainty cultivate fear, whereas honesty brings fear out into the open where it can be handled. Most people would rather know what they have to face than live in the shadowy world of doubt.

Those who work within the hospice movement have often found that people are able, in time, and after the initial trauma, to face the truth about their illness.

When we say, 'He couldn't take it,' we should perhaps change it to, 'I can't take it.' Often our refusal to tell the truth to a dying person reflects *our* struggle not the patient's. A dying person has a far greater capacity to face the truth than we realize. The dying can accept the prospect of death far better than can the living. So we need to be careful that we who are fit and well do not project on to those who are seemingly closer to death the fear that we have. This fear of death may well be more ours than theirs.

The God-given capacity to face up to death should never be underestimated. 'My grace is sufficient for you' (2 Cor 12:9) is a promise for the dying as well as the living.

Who should tell?

The doctor has the knowledge and the authority to share the news of terminal illness with a person. His knowledge and understanding of the diagnosis give weight to his words. His emotional detachment makes it easier for the patient to accept the truth from him. It is important, however, that detachment does not lead to coldness. It should always be hard for a doctor to tell the truth to a dying person, and it is right that the patient senses the doctor's difficulty. Not every doctor is willing to face this responsibility; for some it is tantamount to admitting he has failed. He may have failed to cure, but he need not fail to care. Where doctors put curing before caring, the task of telling the truth to terminally ill patients will be well-nigh impossible.

How to tell?

There is no simple way to tell a person he is going to die. It takes sensitivity and courage. First, listen to what the terminally ill person is saying. His questions may indicate how willing he is to listen to an honest answer. 'I am not going to die, am I?' may reflect fear and an unwillingness to face the truth. So we may judge that it is not yet time to tell. 'Be honest with me, I am not going to get better, am I?' reflects a degree of preparation and a greater willingness to hear the truth.

Secondly, answer the questions dying people are asking. It is the patient who should lead the way on the matter of when to tell the truth, and just how much of the truth to share at the time. On this sensitive issue, Dame Cicely Saunders writes, 'We have to try to learn to give the truth the individual needs that moment in the simplest and kindest way we can offer it, leaving him the choice to take it or leave it as he wishes.'[7]

If, after several attempts to share the truth of his illness with a dying person, it is obvious that the person does not wish to know the truth, or at least to share the truth with us, we should respect his choice. It is wrong to try to force a person to talk about his death; such coercion is impossible anyway.

The dying person will probably be selective when it comes to talking to people about death. He may find he can talk to a nurse, a minister or even a relative stranger much more easily than he can to his own family. This selectivity will be in part due to the pain of speaking to those he loves and in part to a desire not to hurt them. Such careful selection by the dying person should not be misunderstood, especially by the family.

Communication need not always be verbal. The husband catching his wife's glare from the other side of a crowded room knows that! Some of you reading this will be able to identify with the words of this widow, speaking about the knowledge she and her husband shared before his death: 'I knew. He knew. He knew that I knew. I knew that he knew that I knew. And we didn't say a word to each other.'[8] For that couple, words were unnecessary.

Fear of dying

Once a person knows he is dying, what matters most is that he is given hope and reassurance about future treatment and care. Most people are more worried by the process of dying than the fact of death. The unexpressed fear in many a heart is, 'How will I die?' Against the background of honesty, the real and urgent questions of the dying can be voiced. Will there be any pain? Will I feel anything? Will I be alone? Much reassurance can be given to the person who has these questions.

Let those who have had experience in caring for the dying speak. 'Distress in the last hour is rare . . . There is . . . almost always a rather beautiful giving-in. The person withdraws serenely and willingly, as gently as an ocean liner slips away from the quayside.'[9] From within the context of hospice care, Dame Cicely Saunders writes, 'Some have said to me that they hoped "it would be in their sleep", and this is something we can promise with little fear that we will be wrong . . . almost always unconsciousness precedes death.'[10]

Most important of all is the assurance that the Lord who is our shepherd will be with us:

> Even though I walk
> through the valley of the shadow of death,
> I will fear no evil,
> for you are with me;
> your rod and your staff,
> they comfort me.
> (Ps 23:4)

To tell or not to tell? The question haunts the members of a family where one of them is dying. The voice of self-preservation cries 'No'; the voice of faith whispers 'Yes'. Where there is kind and sensitive honesty, what Dr R G Twycross calls 'gentle truth', a door is opened for God to minister his infinite riches to the dying and their families.

After the initial shock, tears and despair, God brings the gifts of faith and courage, and with them a new sense of purpose. The dying and their families, living within the atmosphere of honesty, discover new depths within their relationships both with one another and with God. With God's help we can face the truth about dying and discover that he is 'able to do immeasurably more than all we ask or imagine' (Eph 3:20).

3
'It can't be true!'

'As I stepped out of the doctor's surgery I could not really believe that anything was seriously wrong.'[1] David Watson, in common with most of us, found bad news impossible to handle at first. Others confronted by bad news feel it is a nightmare from which they will wake. 'This is the sort of thing that happens to other people; it can't be happening to me.' In these and other ways we deny, in typical human fashion, that which we are unwilling to accept. But is denial merely a human response?

Denial: a God-given safety valve

Denial is a normal and healthy coping mechanism, giving us time to digest unwelcome news. Denial acts first as a block to bad news getting through and then as a filter allowing the news to seep through gradually until we can handle it all. In this way the defence mechanism of denial acts as a buffer, preventing us from being seriously injured by bad news.

When people first hear about their own terminal illness they deny it in a variety of ways. Some will ask for second and third opinions from the doctors. Others, ostrich-like, will refuse to discuss the bad news, talking instead about future plans, as if a positive view of the future will remove the dark shadow cast over the present. Others will apparently not hear what the doctor has shared with them. Some people will choose to ignore symptoms of terminal illness, referring instead to a flu bug, a chesty cold or a touch of arthritis.

This radical denial of facts in the very early stages of terminal illness is not wrong; it is a God-given safety valve. We should handle other people's denial in a non-committal way, neither playing the game with them nor rebuking them. In this way we lay a foundation for a more honest relationship in the future when the other person is ready for it.

Faith or denial?

Denial can sometimes wear the spiritual mask of faith. Christians are particularly susceptible to confusing faith in God and normal human denial. David Watson conceded the possibility of denial masquerading as faith. On leaving the doctor's surgery having heard that he might have a malignant ulcer, he promptly bought a brief-case for a trip to California planned for the following week. Watson comments on his shopping, '. . . purchasing the brief-case for the journey became for me a symbol of faith. Or was it fear?'[2] He did not go to California the following week, but entered hospital instead.

The confusion between faith and denial sometimes continues after divine healing has been claimed. In some cases the symptoms of the illness get worse but the sufferer is urged to keep believing that he has been healed. To stand at the bedside of a terminally ill person who is racked with pain and urge him to believe that he has been healed is neither biblically justifiable nor spiritually comforting. At best it is wholly irrelevant; at worst it is cruel. If it is continued, the sufferer is left bewildered and isolated. To be open to the glorious possibility of God healing is one thing; to insist that God can do nothing other than heal is quite another. Those who believe that God *always* heals will sometimes find that they are unable to minister to the real needs of a dying person, simply because of their refusal, through 'faith', to recognize those needs. The dying person is then left either holding on to a false hope of healing or chastising himself for his 'weak faith'. More has been said about this important subject in chapter one.

Denial of the approach of death is necessary and helpful initially. Through denial the sufferer buys a little time. It is when that basic denial continues, and especially when it assumes a spiritual guise, that it becomes harmful. This defence mechanism of denial often returns in another helpful form once the initial bad news has been accepted.

'Not-yet denial'

Once the patient or the family have accepted the seriousness of the news about terminal illness, a more moderate expression of denial appears. The patient, having accepted the situation, may react in this way: 'Yes, I know I am dying, but I am not dying yet.' From the acceptance of death the person returns to take up the challenge of living whatever life remains. After a deep acceptance of his own illness, John turned back to life with such vigour that some might have wondered whether in fact he knew he was dying. The denial was not basic, it was functional, enabling him to live. Ruth Kopp stresses the importance of what she calls 'not-yet denial': 'The "not-yet" phase of denial during the course of an individual's fatal illness is an entirely normal, appropriate, and functional progression, not a regression . . . The "not-yet" phase of denial allows the terminally ill individual to go on living and to enjoy the time he has left.'[3] It has been said, 'Neither the sun nor death can be looked at with a steady eye.'[4] People cannot brood about death all the time. Life, however short, is for living. Hence functional denial is a way of saying, 'Business as usual.'

It is this functional denial that can be seen among patients in a hospice, a special home for the care of the dying. Those who have never visited a hospice can be forgiven for imagining that such a place must be filled with gloom and doom. It was with some apprehension that, during my sabbatical, I entered St Christopher's Hospice in South London to begin a four week multi-disciplinary course which included working as an auxiliary nurse on one of the wards. Doom and gloom? My eyes were opened. Many patients were happily engaged in creative activities, at the same time knowing that they had less time than more in which to live. They were not denying the fact of death, but had learnt to live in day-tight compartments, on the assumption that though death was near it was not necessarily coming that day. This kind of denial, 'not-yet' denial, enables the dying person to spend more time in the work room than in the waiting room.

Recognizing the type of denial

Elisabeth Kübler-Ross points out that a terminally ill person will move easily and quickly between acceptance of death and functional denial, or what she terms 'partial denial'. Denial is not a neat stage through which a person passes initially in order to leave it behind them. One moment a dying person may be speaking freely about death and heaven, and then in the next breath talk about future plans. This is quite normal and should neither be misunderstood nor the apparent contradiction exposed, 'the need [for denial] comes and goes, and the sensitive and perceptive listener will acknowledge this and allow the patient his defences without making him aware of the contradictions.'[5] This constant backwards and forwards movement between the overt acceptance of death and a denial of death may account for the different opinions expressed concerning the patient's knowledge of his or her own condition.

Denial is a normal and helpful defence mechanism when used at the appropriate time and in the appropriate manner. It is when denial dons the mask of faith that it becomes a dangerous and unfulfilling game.

4 The pain of dying

What is it like to die? If we are going to bring relevant care to those who are dying, we must have the courage to ask this question. In this chapter we are going to identify some of the feelings of the dying person and then trace the stages through which he might pass before death. However, let it be said at the outset that for each person who dies, and his family, death is a unique experience. Just as our lives are unique so are our deaths.

Loneliness

Dying is the loneliest experience of life. C S Lewis captures this inevitable loneliness poignantly as he describes the diverging roads along which he and his wife walked prior to her death: 'We both knew this. I had my miseries not hers; she had hers, not mine. The ending of hers would be the coming-of-age of mine. We were setting out on different roads. This cold truth, this terrible traffic-regulation ("You, Madam, to the right – you, Sir, to the left") is just the beginning of the separation which is death itself.'[1]

Only those who have watched with a dying person over weeks or months will be able to fully appreciate how diverging are the roads, and how different are the miseries.

While there is no way of completely removing loneliness, there are many practical ways of easing it. When patients die in hospital, they often need the company and conversation of other patients and staff. The single side-room is appropriate only if the family or friends are permitted to spend many hours with the patient. So often the side-room resembles the condemned cell into which no other patients come and staff enter only occasionally. Such isolation must increase loneliness.

On a busy open ward, too, a dying patient can feel desperately alone. The embarrassed looks, the hushed whispers, the superficial joviality, the doctor passing the bed with nothing more than a 'Good morning, how are you today?', all increase the patient's loneliness. One dying woman expressed her feelings in verse:[2]

I huddle warm inside my corner bed,
Watching the other patients sipping tea.
I wonder why I'm so long getting well,
And why it is that no one will talk to me.

The nurses are so kind. They brush my hair
On days I feel too ill to read or sew.
I smile and chat, try not to show my fear,
They cannot tell me what I want to know.

The visitors come in. I see their eyes
Become embarrassed as they pass my bed.
'What lovely flowers', they say, then hurry on
In case their faces show what can't be said.

The chaplain passes on his weekly round
With friendly smile and calm, untroubled brow,
He speaks with deep sincerity of Life.
I'd like to speak of death but don't know how.

The surgeon comes, with student retinue,
Mutters to Sister, deaf to my silent plea.
I want to tell this dread I feel inside,
But they are all too kind to talk to me.

Silence can increase loneliness. Keeping patients in the dark about their illness and the treatment plays havoc with their imaginations. Fears with no basis in solid fact invade the mind, especially at night. Only the gentle sharing of facts can dispel such fears. It is information about the symptoms of their illnesses and the possible side effects of treatment that can bring dying patients out of the lonely cells in which the prospect of death has locked them.

No longer a person

If a patient is not informed or consulted about his illness he can begin to feel he doesn't matter anymore. Has the illness become more important than the person? Whose illness is it? There follows a loss of self-esteem which further increases the loneliness of the dying. Some of the nursing care that has to be given can be an invasion of privacy, undermining the patient's sense of modesty.

An over-scientific approach to illness can be dehumanizing and degrading. This was David Watson's experience during a series of hospital tests and examinations: 'Although I am sure that this was far from the hospital's intention, I *felt* little more than a slab of meat placed before sophisticated scientific instruments for the benefit of measuring disease. I was no longer a person with human emotions, fears and forebodings, struggling to maintain some positive hope.'[3] The dying are people, not guinea pigs.

Some weeks before his death, I visited John in hospital. Both his arms were in splints, a saline drip into one arm, a blood transfusion into the other. He was unable to scratch his nose, reach for a glass of water or grab a bowl in which to be sick. His helplessness was appalling. I remembered a description of Jesus before his crucifixion, 'They bound him' (John 18:12). Those active hands were soon to be nailed to a cross. Thank God he knows what helplessness is all about.

Fear

A multitude of fears attack the minds of dying people. There are the fears of pain, of weakness, of mental and physical deterioration, and of mutilation through surgery. There is the fear of something happening when you are alone and no one being on hand to help. There is the fear of becoming dependent upon others, of being a 'nuisance'. People are afraid the family will not be able to cope as their illness progresses. There is the fear of entering hospital. Jane Zorza, who died of cancer at the age of twenty-three, wrote in her diary about the 'horrors' that came over her especially at night. All she could think of was the cancer eating away at the healthy parts of her body.[4]

Guilt

The dying person may experience different levels of guilt. On a superficial level he may feel guilty about 'causing so much trouble'. Constant and loving reassurance is needed then. Going deeper, he may feel guilty about not going to the doctor sooner. Deeper still there may be guilt about past sins that have never been confessed or for which assurance of forgiveness has never been received.

Those caring for the dying must discern between false and true guilt. False guilt must be handled patiently and positively. True guilt must be confessed and brought to Jesus Christ. On the basis of scripture we can give assurance that the blood of Jesus goes on cleansing us from all sin (1 John 1:7). John Stott writes of this verse, 'The verb suggests that God does more than forgive; He erases the stain of sin. And the present tense shows that it is a continuous process.'[5] The great blessing awaiting the 'cleansed heart' is seeing God (Matt 5:8).

Sadness and despair

There are times when the dying will experience deep sadness about the unfinished business of life and the carefully-made plans that illness will not allow to come to fruition. They experience a living grief that is most strongly felt in relation to their families, whom they love and do not want to leave. Of all the pains of dying, this, for many, is the most acute. It was so for John.

For the family, bereavement does not begin after death; it begins the moment the terminal nature of an illness is accepted. Loved ones and friends start their grieving while the dying person is still alive.

Despair takes root when the dying, or their families, feel that nothing can be done. If there is the awareness that the illness cannot be cured and, furthermore, that nothing can be done to alleviate distressing symptoms such as pain, nausea and breathlessness, then despair takes over.

While despair should never be lifted by false hope, it can be lifted by the assurance of skilful, attentive and personal care. As far as the symptoms of terminal illness are concerned, there is *always* something that can be done. Dame Cicely Saunders captures several facets of real caring when she speaks of the approach of hospice staff to a new patient: 'You matter because you are you. You matter to the last moment of your life, and we will do all we can not only to help you die peacefully, but also to live until you die.'[6]

The five stages

Dr Elisabeth Kübler-Ross, one of the foremost authorities on the care of the dying, has identified five stages through which the terminally ill may pass. Here is a brief outline of these stages, or coping mechanisms. The first two, denial and anger, are dealt with more fully in chapters three and twelve of this book.

Denial – 'No, not me!'

The initial reaction on learning that you are dying is simply not to believe it. 'It can't be true. This only happens to other people.' This is a necessary first response that is usually temporary, being replaced gradually by acceptance.

Anger – 'Why me?'

Numb denial is followed by aggressive indignation. Why shouldn't a dying person feel anger? Kübler-Ross shares her insight into this anger:

> Maybe we too would be angry if all our life activities were interrupted so prematurely; if all the buildings we started were to go unfinished, to be completed by someone else; if we had put some hard earned money aside to enjoy a few years of rest and enjoyment, for travel and pursuing hobbies, only to be confronted with the fact that 'this is not for me'.

Kübler-Ross further suggests that the patient, in being angry, may be saying, 'I am alive, don't forget that. You can hear my voice, I am not dead yet!'[7]

Bargaining – 'Yes, it is me, but . . .'

At this stage the person knows that time is short but

wants an extension of life for a particular reason – a wedding, a graduation, a visit from a friend living abroad, a last holiday, a last Christmas. The reasons are multiple, the bargaining normal.

Depression

The word 'depression', used in this context, is an umbrella word under which a variety of emotions shelter – regret, guilt, grief, helplessness. At this stage there is a deep sadness at the loss of so much, and an overwhelming feeling of helplessness in the face of death.

The pathway to the acceptance of death winds in and out of the valley of depression. This depression is a normal part of the grieving of a dying person who is losing everything and everyone he loves. It is characterized by moodiness and silence. The most helpful response of visitors to this stage may also be a loving silence, and a meaningful squeeze of the hand. The patient should not be encouraged to 'snap out of it', for that is tantamount to telling him not to face his own death. Too many visitors at this stage hinder the emotional preparation that the dying person is making; the number of visitors should therefore be controlled.

Acceptance – 'Yes'

This is a state of positive surrender, rather than stoic resignation. It is the 'Rise! Let us go!' (Mark 14:42) of Jesus in Gethsemane. The patient accepts that the struggle is over, the time is short and the 'time of departure is at hand'. This stage is almost devoid of feelings. This is also the time when the family needs much support, perhaps more than the patient himself. The dying person's circle of interest has shrunk: the TV is off, the weather outside is irrelevant, family decisions concern him no longer; all these things belong to the world he is preparing to leave. To give attention to them would mean grasping again that which he has struggled to let go. Families and friends need to be sensitive to this stage and not misinterpret it as signifying a lack of love on the part of the dying. Communication with the patient will be more non-verbal than verbal, and visits should be shorter and more limited.

There are two important qualifications that need to be added to these five so-called stages. First, not every dying person experiences each one of these stages, either because there is insufficient time or, more probably, because one or other of the stages is irrelevant for that particular person. Second, a person does not move from one stage into the next in a neat, distinguishable progression. A dying person may move in and out of these stages at different times. The stages should be regarded as signposts along the road being travelled by the dying and indicators of the kind of understanding and care needed at a particular time.

Prepare now

We have been looking at the feelings of a dying person and the stages that can sometimes be recognized, with a view to helping someone else, a loved one or friend to 'die well'. But what about ourselves? How will we face the end of life? In the *Dictionary of Medical Ethics*, Tom S West writes of the way man faces death:

> His ability to face the end of his life on this earth may spring from the manner in which that life has been led. Faith or courage or love do not often make their first appearance at the death bed. However, if such virtues have at least been recognized during a man's lifetime it is often at the time of his dying that their reality and strength are revealed. All our lives we are preparing for death.[8]

5
The care of the dying

In the last chapter we attempted to enter the mind of a dying person in order to understand what he feels. What a mixture of emotions wage war there – fear, guilt, anger, a sense of worthlessness, frustration and sadness. An intolerable battle? 'Suffering is only intolerable when nobody cares' (Dame Cicely Saunders). Now we must face the challenge to care for the dying.[1] Included in that challenge must be the care of the carers, whose needs, though different, are often as great as the needs of the dying.

Dying at home

The wind of change

Earlier this century, people were more familiar with death and dying. The shadow of death was more often cast over a home than it is today, often claiming a baby or a child. Furthermore, because more people died at home, our grandparents were more acquainted with the *ars moriendi*, the art of dying, and the practical skills needed to care for the dying.

Today, many people have never witnessed a death or seen a dead body. Death and dying have been removed from the home and transferred to the hospital. Now the primary carers are the professionals, and the family are relegated to a secondary caring role, or worse, that of passive spectators. As a result, people are frightened of the dying and feel inadequate when it comes to caring for them.

However, the wind of change is blowing. Increasingly the home is being seen as the best place in which to care for the dying. Most people, in fact, would prefer to die at home. In his classic work, *Dying*, John Hinton wrote:

> Dying persons gain so much more by being cared for by an affectionate family; they are better able to maintain themselves as individuals. Remaining at home, not swallowed up in the possible anonymity of the dying hospital patient, they need not doubt they are still part of the family. While among their family, they do not consider themselves as hulks awaiting the end, as long as they can participate, even in a limited role.[2]

The hospice movement is campaigning for the care of the dying to centre on the home whenever possible. In the future the family and the medical profession will work together more as a team, with the experts functioning in an advisory and supportive role and the family and friends being the primary carers in the home.

While this may well be the direction in which the care of the dying should move, there are factors in our society militating against its unqualified success. The family unit is more fragmented today, so that a family may be scattered, with different members living in different parts of the world. More significantly, the family unit is under strain in the western world. Old loyalties and commitments no longer exist. Not all children are prepared or able to take responsibility for the care of their parents and grandparents. The recognition of the disintegration of the family unit in the west may expose a degree of unrealistic idealism in the views of the hospice movement.

Nevertheless, caring for the dying at home will

increase in the future. As Christians who believe that the family unit is God's idea we should be in the front line of this advance towards more home care.

Supporting the carers at home

The care of the dying at home imposes a great strain on those doing the caring, especially when the caring becomes long-term. Maximum support for the family is essential. That support can come from a variety of sources, professional and voluntary, and through a variety of means, ranging from expert nursing to meals on wheels. Unfortunately the services and facilities available vary considerably in different parts of the country. The local authorities are legally obliged to provide nursing care at home for those who need it. They may also provide many other services.

The general practitioner is the key figure, the person who can open the door for other helpers to enter the home where a family is caring for someone who is dying. Through the family doctor, contact can be made with two other key persons – the district nurse and the health visitor. The district nurse comes to work with the patient and the family; the health visitor comes to advise the patient and the family on a number of matters, not all of which are directly medical. Between them, the doctor, the district nurse and the health visitor can put the family in touch with all the different services available in the area. They can advise on night calls from a nurse and a 'sitter service', providing people, both qualified and unqualified, to sit with the patient through the night, thereby allowing the members of the family to get some needed sleep. Through the Social Services, home-help may be provided and in some districts there is a laundry service for bed linen. Through voluntary agencies meals may be provided.

Financial help may also be available to families caring for a seriously ill person. The DHSS can advise about an attendance allowance, and the Cancer Relief Organization supply grants in some instances to those nursing a person suffering from cancer.

The general practitioner will give advice on additional medical care that might be available in the area such as Macmillan nurses, Marie Curie hospitals and hospices. There are also private nursing agencies whose resources may be tapped.

In many areas there is a wide range of equipment available, including different types of beds, commodes, bed-pans, aids for incontinence, wheelchairs, sheepskins and back-rests.

The support of friends

In spite of all the help that can come from outside sources, the chief responsibility of caring for a dying person at home will fall on the members of the family or very close friends. It is as important to visit the carers as it is to visit the sick person. The sensitive visitor will be willing to listen as the carers talk about their loved one, express their fears, give vent to their anger and share their sadness. Do not overlook the need to care for the carers.

From time to time those looking after the dying person will need to be relieved of the practical demands of caring so that normal daily routines and social activities can be maintained. The children must be taken to school, the shopping must be done and some social contact with friends must be sustained. The carers need to do these things while trusted friends take over the caring for a limited time. Though the dying need preparation for the next world, the carers need preparing for continuing life in this world. 'Getting back to normal' after a bereavement will be that much easier if some of life's normal routine has been maintained throughout the time of caring for the dying.

Not everyone can die at home

Although to die at home may be the preference of the majority of people, and also the direction in which terminal care is moving at this time, it is not appropriate for every individual or family. If the dying person doubts the ability of the family to cope, he will prefer hospital, feeling safer there. The nature of the illness, and the fact of symptoms not being under control, may necessitate hospitalization.

Sometimes the family situation makes it impossible for them to look after a dying person. An elderly wife has promised her husband that she will nurse him to the end. Exhausted and failing in health, she finds she is unable to keep her promise, and reluctantly agrees to her husband entering hospital. Then guilt holds the wife in its grip: 'I will never forgive myself for putting him in hospital,' she cries in anguish. She need not feel guilty, in spite of the broken promise. She knows that she let her husband go into hospital because she loved him and wanted him to have the care she was unable to give. The Lord looks at the wife's dilemma of love and understands.

Caring through listening

Love listens

One of the most significant ministries that can be given to the dying is that of listening. Nothing lifts loneliness like quiet, loving listening. Nothing exorcizes the ghosts of fear more effectively than talking to a good listener. Listening gives worth and respect to a person, restoring shattered self-esteem. Frustration, tension and anger all need to be released into words. It is the listener who gives permission to the dying and their families to 'fire away'. The dying need the company of those who love them. Love listens.

'You've helped so much!'

I am sure you have had the experience of being thanked for help you were quite unaware of giving. You gave no profound advice and shared no inspired insight. In fact, you hardly got a word in edgeways; yet you are being thanked for your help! What help? You listened! The Lord has given us two ears and one mouth and yet we act as though the proportion were reversed.

When someone is listening, the speaker has the opportunity to set out his ideas and problems and so to look at them more clearly. When this is done, the problem may shrink and assume a more realistic size, or a solution may be seen by the speaker himself. The listener has been a sounding board, and the atmosphere of listening has been immensely productive. What the active listener has done is to enable the speaker to see and solve his own problem. The problem of fear especially needs to be put into words. Fear has a way of disappearing when it is expressed.

Ten guidelines to listening

- *Listen with concentration*. Keep your mind actively engaged in what is being said, not on what you are going to say next.
- *Listen with stillness*. Don't fidget, stifle a yawn or sneak a glance at your watch.
- *Listen without interrupting*. Don't say, 'I remember when . . .' In good listening there is *no* room for reminiscences.
- *Listen without giving pat answers*. The friends of Job did a great work when they sat in silence with him for seven days and seven nights. Then they made a mistake. They started talking! Never be afraid to admit that you do not know the answers, especially to the mystery of suffering. It is better to share the darkness and bewilderment of a dying person than

to provide irrelevant answers.

- *Listen without judging*. Be a 'safe' person on whom the dying and the family can vent their hurts, without fear of being condemned or causing you offence.
- *Listen with your eyes*. Watch for the signs of agitation in the speaker. His body language may speak louder than his words.
- *Show you are listening*. Do so by your eyes, a nod of the head and the occasional encouraging word.
- *Don't be afraid of silences*. Silence can provide a time to reflect for both listener and speaker. Silence can also give the opportunity for the listener to empathize, to climb into the skin of the speaker and feel his feelings. There is no real listening without empathy.
- *Don't pry*. Do not trespass on the private land of the speaker's life. He must decide which gates he opens for you.
- *Listen and reflect back*. 'What I think you are saying is . . .' This reflecting back enables you to convey your listening, and to establish how accurate it has been. It enables the speaker to correct where you have misunderstood and, more important, to hear his thoughts from someone else.

Listening requires discipline and must be learnt. The more you think you know, the harder it is to listen. Ask anyone involved in counselling! The wise person learns to listen. 'It is the province of knowledge to speak, and it is the privilege of wisdom to listen.'[3]

If you are seeking to help someone who is very ill or to support a family coping with terminal illness or to offer friendship to someone in bereavement, ask God to give you a listening heart. Remember the God whom you are asking is the great listener. To listen is therefore to reflect his character.

Caring through prayer

'I can't pray!'

There are times when a seriously ill person finds it difficult, if not impossible, to pray. Even those with a long-established, disciplined prayer life may experience this difficulty. This can be disturbing, causing the person to wonder whether he is losing his faith, and distressing, making him feel he has sinned.

It is important to understand the cause of this prayerlessness. The cause is rooted in the illness and not the spiritual life of the individual. For example, when a person is suffering chronic pain, that pain 'fills the universe'. It absorbs all energy, leaving none with which to cope with other challenges. The patient will not wish to eat, get up, see visitors or be bothered with anything. The pain has his undivided attention. For the same reason he will not be able to pray.

At these times of prayer difficulty, John Bunyan's words bring comfort, 'The best prayers have been more groans than words.' The apostle Paul also assures us that God's ability to understand and answer our prayers does not depend on our ability to express those prayers. The Holy Spirit within us knows our hearts and presents our prayers before the throne of God (Rom 8:26,27).

Praying with the dying

The dying person needs Christian friends to pray with him, especially when he feels unable to pray himself. Such prayers should be brief, honest and relevant. Some aspect of an earlier conversation can be taken up in prayer. A fear that has been expressed can be brought before God. The family and medical staff should be included in the prayer. The greatest concern of the dying is usually members of the family. These people should be brought by name before God and commended to his care. Pray about the symptoms of the patient's illness. To pray with the laying-on of hands may be particularly appropriate when praying about the symptoms.

Some will find solace in the Collects in the Prayer Book or in one of the prayers used in the service of Holy Communion. When a person is agonizing over the will of God, the 'Serenity Prayer' of Reinhold Niebuhr could be helpful:

> God grant me the serenity
> to accept the things I cannot change;
> courage to change the things I can;
> and wisdom to know the difference.

Praying for the dying

The church has a responsibility to pray for the terminally ill and their families. Constant assurance, 'We are praying for you,' needs to be given. However, that can sound glib. It is helpful when the promise to pray can be demonstrated, as for example, through a prayer vigil. In a prayer vigil, a group of friends feel burdened to pray. Each of them chooses a certain hour or time during the day (and night) when they will commit themselves to specific prayer for a friend who is seriously ill and for his family. Their names and the times are listed, and each intercessor has the list, as do the family and the friend who is sick. It is the quality of fellowship that makes the prayer vigil very special for the dying person and his family.

A prayer chain is a further way of demonstrating fellowship in prayer. One person acts as a contact with the family. On a daily basis, or in the event of a crisis, the family telephone their contact who in turn telephones the next person on the chain, and so on. Those on the prayer chain must be willing to be contacted at any time, day or night.

The fellowship of prayer is a marvellous source of strength to the dying and their families. To know, for sure, that you are being prayed for, means so much. We should not hesitate to be practical and organized in providing this quality of support and fellowship.

Caring through the use of scripture

Those caring for the dying and their families will search the scriptures for an appropriate word. We should remember the importance of the familiar when ministering to the seriously ill from the Bible. Their favourite translation, the one they know and love, is the one from which we should read.

A phrase

The seriously ill are not able to concentrate for long time spans. Any reading of the Bible should therefore be brief. One verse is often what is needed, a truth to hold for a little while. A senior missionary kept repeating one phrase during the last few days of her life: 'Nothing shall separate us'. It was not only difficult to plant another verse in her mind, it was unnecessary; God gave her the truth she needed.

A picture

One afternoon in hospital, John and I read the story of Jesus walking on the water (Mark 6:45–52). We focused our thoughts on the initiative Jesus took and the path he trod. Then we pictured Jesus taking the same initiative that afternoon and walking down the corridor and into the room where John was lying. Jesus was still the master of the waves and storms, still the one who climbed in beside his troubled children, still the bringer of peace. Looking at that story from the gospels in that way enabled us not only to say, 'There was Jesus,' but, 'Here comes Jesus!'

An action

A biblical truth can be brought home by a simple action. Sometimes when I am speaking to a person about the keeping power of God, I take their hand and hold it firmly. Then I ask them to take their hand away, at the same time not letting them do so. I then read some verses from the Bible which remind us that God's grip upon us is infinitely stronger (John 10:28,29; Rom 8:38,39).

Caring during the last hours

To care for someone right up to the moment they leave this life is a very special privilege. To those who have never experienced ministering in this way it may seem a daunting prospect. Do not be afraid. There is a strength that God gives that surpasses our highest thought. During the last hours of a person's life God's strength is perfected in the weakness of the carers. To continue to care for someone right to the end is demanding but immensely enriching. God does not fail either the dying or the carers.

Even when the dying person is asleep or unconscious, it is essential that someone is with him. During the last hours learn stillness. Don't fuss or talk too much. Maintain physical contact with the person by holding his hand and speaking occasional words of assurance. Little actions like wiping the forehead and moistening the lips are so relevant at this time.

Be careful to avoid whispered conversations at the bedside, even when a person is unconscious. Hearing is one of the last faculties to fail. Though unable to communicate, the dying person may nevertheless be able to hear what people are saying, as awareness may remain when response is gone.

What happens at death?

The question uppermost in the minds of both the dying person and those doing the caring is, 'How will death come?' Unless some attempt is made to answer that question, people are prey to all kinds of fears and fantasies, particularly to the fear that death is accompanied by overwhelming pain. In fact 'pain nearly always subsides just before the end; the patient feels an overwhelming drowsiness and dies in his sleep'.[4]

As a person approaches death there are certain signs that can sometimes be discerned. Often the level of unconsciousness deepens. The pattern of breathing alters, stopping momentarily and starting again. Fluid gathering in the chest may cause a rattling sound. Eventually the moment is reached when the last breath is taken. The muscles relax and the heart stops. The moment of death is usually quiet and peaceful.

What is to be done after death?

If the person dies at home, certain practical steps should be taken. Excess bedding should be removed, leaving just one pillow. The body should be laid straight. The eyelids should be closed and the mouth held closed by placing a suitable object under the chin. The fingers should be straightened. Heating should be turned off in the room. The doctor should be informed immediately death has taken place. He will come to verify the death and to issue the death certificate. The washing of the body is nowadays usually done by the funeral director who should be contacted after the doctor has confirmed the death. However a member of the family may well feel that the washing of the body is a final ministry they would like to fulfil.

God's care of the dying

The Holy Spirit's ministry

During John's last two days, meaningful conversation had virtually ceased. Under heavy sedation, John slept most of the time. Suddenly John began speaking in his sleep. He seemed to be leading a meeting, something he had done many times. He invited people to join him in prayer. The phrases he repeated several times in the prayer were, 'Father, let your name be honoured' and 'Father, let your name be glorified'.

Although the painful memories of John's last days have not totally disappeared, even after several years, I have the deep conviction that God ministered to John in a way that no person could at that time. When response from the dying person is minimal or absent we feel that they have drifted beyond our reach. But they have not drifted beyond the reach of God, their shepherd who is walking every step of the valley of the shadow of death with them.

The Holy Spirit ministers Christ. Mrs Stokes was an elderly lady who came to faith in Jesus Christ a few months before she died of cancer. One night in hospital, she suffered a massive haemorrhage and excruciating pain. When I spoke to her the following day, just a matter of hours before she died, she was calm and told me how, in the midst of her agony the previous night, she had thought of Jesus' sufferings on the cross, and how much greater they must have been than hers. The Holy Spirit had ministered Christ to her at the moment of her greatest need. In our caring for the dying, we are but servants of the divine carer, God himself.

Jesus Christ . . . more than sufficient

During his last illness, a retired Bible College principal was visited by one of his former students. The old teacher, speaking of the past, explained how he had laid great emphasis in all his teaching on the importance of the will. Viewing that past emphasis in the light of his present physical weakness, the principal realized that he had not allowed for the close connection between the will and the physical condition of the body. For in his present physical weakness he had neither the strength nor the will to read his Bible. He therefore found no satisfaction in his will. He continued, 'When a man reaches the stage where I am, nothing will satisfy him but the sheer free grace of God in Jesus Christ. And I am finding that more than sufficient.'[5]

6
Death with dignity

'We are prevented from dying, we are not helped to live';[1] 'You matter because you are you. You matter to the last moment of your life, and we will do all we can not only to help you die peacefully, but also to live until you die.'[2] Two quotations from two different worlds. The first comes from a dying patient in a hospital. He is being kept alive, but at a cost – his quality of life. The second comes from the world of the hospice. It is an example of the way new patients are welcomed. The shadow of death hovers unmistakably over both worlds, a dark shadow over the one, a brighter shadow over the other.

The world of the hospice

My sabbatical enquiry into the care of the dying took me into the world of the hospice, for me a totally new one. I found myself part of a community that was highly professional and deeply caring. The atmosphere was somewhere between that of hospital and home, a little nearer the latter than the former.

As we move into the world of the hospice in this chapter, we will be looking at principles of care that are appropriate for all carers, irrespective of where they happen to be doing the caring. Hospice care travels well. These principles can be applied at home by members of the family, or in hospital by staff and family together. If you are looking after someone who is seriously ill, there is much for you to learn from the world of the hospice.

Derivation

In the Middle Ages there were hospices all over Europe, based in the monasteries and catering for the needs of pilgrims. They were places where the tired could find refreshment and shelter and where the injured could be nursed back to health before continuing their journey. The hospice was essentially a 'shelter for travellers'.

It was not until the late nineteenth century that the word 'hospice' took on a narrower meaning, being applied specifically to the care of the dying. The beginning of the modern hospice movement goes back only as far as 1967 with the opening of St Christopher's Hospice in South London. Dame Cicely Saunders was the inspiration behind St Christopher's, and is regarded by many as the pioneer of the modern hospice movement. She traces the modern hospice back to its roots in the Middle Ages: 'Hospice is about a special kind of living and in a sense is still concerned with travelling: patients, families, elderly residents and the staff and volunteers who meet them, find they are drawn into a journey of the spirit.'[3] Death is seen as a crucial stage in a journey, not a terminus.

Definition

A modern hospice has been defined as, 'a skilled community working to improve the quality of life remaining for their patients and their families struggling with mortal and long-term illness'.[4] Phrases such as 'dying with dignity', 'dying well', 'living to the end' are frequently used within the context of hospice care and encapsulate the aims of the hospice movement. Its growth in Europe, the USA and Great Britain since the 1960s has been phenomenal. There are over seventy hospices in Britain at the present time, with many more being planned.

Development

At the heart of the word 'hospice' are ideas and attitudes, not buildings and institutions. Hospice care indicates a certain quality of care, not the particular building in which the care is given. In fact separate buildings are not essential to hospice care. Four different models of hospice may be identified.[5]

St Christopher's was the first of the modern *free-standing hospices*. They are built very largely as a result of the enthusiastic work of people who have captured a vision for hospice care. They are charitable organizations, relying heavily upon the gifts of friends of the hospice. These hospices offer a variety of services in addition to providing beds on the premises for the terminally ill. There may be a day care centre with facilities for physiotherapy and occupational therapy. There may be a domiciliary service providing home visits by nurses to patients living within a certain radius of the hospice. Bereavement counselling of families after a death is a further service offered. Some hospices have teaching programmes for their own staff and multi-disciplinary courses for members of other disciplines – social workers and theological students. Many hospices of this model are engaged in research. The main advantage of this model of hospice care is the community atmosphere which is loving and supportive, an atmosphere tingling with life and reflecting 'hope based in reality'.

The *continuing care unit* is a hospice unit built within the grounds of a hospital, or it may even be a special ward within the hospital. The National Society for Cancer Relief often builds such units. The distinct advantage of this model is its ability to complement the work of the hospital, as doctors are able to move between both. Furthermore, costs can be reduced as facilities and equipment are shared. Many within the hospice movement are zealous in working for a more integrated system of care, and long for the day when hospice principles are part of the thinking and practice of every local hospital.

Another expression of hospice is *home care*. Specially trained nurses work alongside the family doctor and the district nurse in the homes of the terminally ill. These nurses have no back-up beds, no hospice building to which the patient can go if caring becomes impossible at home. The advantage of this model is the way the family are the primary carers supported by the professionals.

Hospital support teams enter hospitals to visit individual patients at the invitation of the hospital. This model is similar to the continuing care unit but goes one step further towards the integration of principles of terminal care into general medical practice.

Different though the four models may be, they are expressions of the same vision. Those working within any of the hospice models share the same insights into terminal care and are fired by the same enthusiasm to share those insights. Hospice care is not a jealously-guarded secret into which the chosen few can be initiated but an open secret to be shared with everyone. Dame Cicely Saunders is in no doubt about the direction the hospice movement must take if it is to benefit the maximum number of people: 'Home Care and Hospital Teams working together in the general NHS seem to be the main way to bring hospice care to the greatest possible number of patients and families in today's situation.'[6]

The hospice emphasis

Fundamental to the special care offered by the hospice is the willingness to change from giving aggressive treatment aiming at cure, to palliative treatment aiming at quality of life. It is this decision that some within the medical profession seem unwilling to make. As a result, futile attempts to cure, attempts that everyone knows will fail, are continued, bringing increased suffering and false hope to patients.

The decision to change the nature of a patient's treatment is a very difficult one. To give up the attempt to cure and to concentrate solely on care requires medical knowledge, courage and compassion. Why are some doctors unwilling to stop aggressive treatment?

Dr R G Twycross considers that the basic orientation of modern medicine militates against good care of the dying: 'In recent years medicine has become so orientated towards prevention and cure that the dying patient is regarded as a failure.'[7]

It could also be that some doctors adopt too rigid a view of the basic aim of medicine, 'to save life'. Saving life must include the easing of suffering and the improving of the patient's quality of life as well as preventing death. With this fuller understanding of the aim of medicine, doctors would be able more readily to switch from cure to care.

The decision to stop aggressive treatment is therefore not a negative, end-of-the-road, fatalistic one, but a positive, loving affirmation that life, however short, can continue. Margaret Manning discusses the doctor's dilemma in switching from cure to care and concludes succinctly, 'Admitting that a patient cannot be cured is not the doctor's fault, but refusing to allow the patient truly to live with that incurable disease, would be.'[8]

In hospice care, attention is focused on treating the symptoms of an illness, the conclusion that the disease is incurable having already been drawn. The symptoms of terminal illness are what cause so much distress, symptoms such as pain, vomiting, and breathlessness. Constipation is another feature that causes far more worry for many sick people than the illness itself, yet it is almost inevitable since it is the side effect of many pain-killing drugs. However, all these symptoms can be treated and in most cases removed completely. That is the good news of hospice care.

What do *you* think is the most relevant treatment that can be offered to a dying person? An expert in the care of the dying is in no doubt about his answer: 'To provide the dying with masses of hospital equipment and drugs and no love is like offering a pot of gold to a starving man buried in sovereigns.'[9] It is compassionate care, focusing on symptom control, that provides relevant, realistic hope for the dying.

Hospice principles

The individual

In hospice care each patient is regarded as a unique person. The patient is not the 'rectal carcinoma' in the second bed; he is Fred Smith, aged fifty-five, a married man with two children, and he is frightened to die. Fred is not a child who must submit passively to the decisions made by the professionals. He is an adult human being who should be informed and consulted at every stage of his illness. Only by constant communication between Fred and the medical staff will the patient be able to maintain some measure of control over his treatment and thereby preserve his own self-esteem.

Communication is a key word in hospice care, communication between the staff and communication with the patient. Daily or twice-daily ward meetings involving all the staff of a hospice ward ensure that everyone knows exactly what developments may have taken place in the condition or care of each patient. Each patient is discussed by name at these meetings. Members of staff, even the most junior, are encouraged to share any insight they might have received following conversations with patients.

Sensitive, loving attempts are made to help the patient understand the nature of his illness and treatment. Communication takes time. Because of the high patient/staff ratio in a hospice there is more time for the staff to sit and listen to and talk with patients. So much of the loneliness of dying is eased if there are those who will spend time listening or just sitting with a patient. To sit quietly holding the hand of a seriously ill person is to communicate love and stillness.

When caring for the dying, it is important not to take away from them their right to make choices. It is misguided love that does everything for the dying. It may well be that the field of choices is a small one, no bigger than the room in which the patient is sitting. Even then the right of the individual to choose is important. The patient should choose where the flowers should be put, how the pillows should be arranged, whether the curtains should be drawn and all the other seemingly insignificant decisions related to his comfort. These small decisions are very important decisions when your world has shrunk to the size of a bedroom.

Hospice care pays attention to detail. A person's self-esteem is often closely linked to their appearance. Morale can be lifted by such mundane things as clothing that fits, a good shave for the men, a hair-do for the women. There is always room for creative, personal caring. Two of the nurses caring for Jane Zorza went out into the fields to gather 'smells'. Picking a variety of plants they took the bunch back to Jane who held each plant to her nose, her eyes shut, as she tried to identify each one. Later the nurses brought in a bunch of herbs for Jane to identify, many of which Jane had used in cooking. 'Each carried many memories. It was as if she was saying goodbye to old friends with whom she had shared good times.'[10]

To really care for the terminally ill is costly. In a

hospice, staff are encouraged to build relationships with individual patients, listening to them, laughing with them, crying with them. There is no room for self-preservation and cold detachment in hospice care; love is at the heart of that care, and love gets involved and is willing to be vulnerable. The staff in a hospice grieve when a patient they loved dies.

It was this emphasis on the individual and the willingness to be vulnerable that so impressed me about hospice care. That is the way God cares too, concentrating upon the individual and exposing himself to suffering. It was supremely expressed in the pattern of Jesus' life of love.

The whole person

Man is more than a body. Man has a body, a mind and a soul, or to put it in terms of needs, man has physical, emotional and spiritual needs. These areas are not separate compartments that can be treated in isolation from one another. Hospice care realizes that pain is more than merely physical. Physical pain is eased or aggravated by a person's state of mind and his spiritual health. Anxiety increases pain. If a patient is watching the clock to see if he can survive pain-free until the next injection is due, his pain will almost certainly increase and be all the more stubborn in responding to treatment.

Hospice care concentrates on pain control and recognizes that pain may be rooted in the physical condition, or linked with fears, depression or grief, or any other of the emotional traumas associated with dying. The pain may also be linked with guilt, regret about past sin, or anger towards God. Ministry from God's word and prayer may provide the answer to the patient's pain.

There is one simple, yet remarkably effective principle adopted by the hospice in relation to the control of physical pain. Pain must be conquered *before* it begins, not once it has started. The next pain-killer must be given *before* the effect of the previous one has worn off. 'Pain control is not so much a matter of what is in the medicine, as it is of how and when it is administered.'[11]

This treatment of the whole person was so much a feature of our Lord's ministry. People's physical, emotional and spiritual needs were, and still are, important to him. Christ loved and died for people, not disembodied souls.

The family

When one person in a family is dying, the whole family suffers, and the whole family needs care. The dying person is travelling a different road, but the signposts are similar. That is why in hospice care there is such a strong emphasis on the family. Hospice care is for the family as well as the patient.

In a hospice, members of the family are encouraged to share in the basic caring. This is important for the family, who otherwise feel so helpless in the face of terminal illness. To be able to share in the caring of your loved one is to begin the task of letting go. The staff see it as part of their responsibility to get to know the family; they are not only preparing a patient for death, but his family as well. That is why after death has occurred, visitors will go from the hospice to offer comfort and counsel to the family. The family's journey can also be a long one, so these visits may be sustained over a period of time.

Christians believe that the family was God's plan and that the family remains the God-given unit for a stable and healthy society. In a culture in which that unit is crumbling, it is heartening to see the hospice movement directing its care to the individual, in all his need, within the context of his family.

The hospice answer to euthanasia

There are those who argue in favour of mercy-killing or euthanasia. One of the arguments is based on the idea that the chronically sick and dying should not be permitted to suffer and that a way out should be available.

A way out is available, not through the door of euthanasia but through the door of hospice care. Dame Cicely Saunders, a dedicated opponent of legalized euthanasia, argues: 'As pain can nearly always be controlled, as both body and mind can be made comfortable while the patient remains alert and fully himself, euthanasia as an escape from physical pain simply should not be necessary.'[12]

So alive!

After the first day working on the ward at St Christopher's, I found myself asking the question: 'Are all these men dying?' Was this an absurd question to ask in a hospice? It is true that within the next few weeks there were to be several deaths, with the inevitable accompanying sadness. Yet the question arose out of the fact that most of the patients on the ward were out of bed, dressed, alert and happy. Everyone was so alive. There was nothing morbid about the work, no air of gloom and doom hovering over the ward. The compassion of the staff was heart-warming, and the courage of the patients was challenging. Working in that atmosphere for a short while was exhilarating. The shadow of death had become brighter.

7
The funeral

In the morning, Jesus stood on the shore
(John 21:4)[1]

Within hours of a death, the family must begin the practical preparations for the funeral. At a time when the mind is numb with grief, decisions have to be made relating to the funeral. The family needs to be well supported at this time, but not over-protected. It is painful to plan and attend the funeral service of one whom you love deeply, but there is a healing component in that pain. It is necessary pain; it is helpful pain; it is healing pain.

Support for the immediate family circle can come from another member of the family or a friend who has had experience of attending to the practical matters of registering a death and arranging a funeral. The funeral director is a professional who will give clear and sensitive advice. Many funeral directors will provide a leaflet outlining the decisions that must be made and the authorities that must be notified. One such is the DHSS leaflet, 'What To Do After A Death' (see appendix).

Viewing the body

Together with the funeral, the viewing of the body after death is almost the only other death ritual left in our culture. There are times when viewing the body is essential to the acceptance of death. Following a sudden death, when the mind reacts with deep shock and total numbness, viewing the body can break the hold of shock and sensitize numbness. When relatives are living away from home and have not seen the deceased for some time, seeing the body may help them to grasp the reality of what has happened. If the last time the person was seen alive he was in hospital wired up to machinery, it may be helpful to see the body in a more dignified and peaceful state.

Margaret's mother died in hospital following a fire in the mother's flat. The daughter's last memory of her mother was of a charred body fighting for life, a horrific memory. It was a great comfort for Margaret a few days later to view her mother's body in the quiet of the funeral parlour. There was no smell of burning and the basic embalming done by the funeral director had almost removed the burn marks.

Equally there are times, as for example when the body has been seriously maimed in death, when viewing the body may be wholly inappropriate.

It is the *thought* of viewing the dead body that people find frightening. The reality is usually easier. Within the peaceful surroundings of a funeral parlour or the more intimate atmosphere of the family home, and following the basic hygienic treatment given by the funeral director, the body usually appears 'at rest'. You are left with the overwhelming impression that the real person has vacated the body, and that the body, after death, is an empty shell.

If a person wants to view the body, but is frightened, this fear can be overcome by a friend or the minister talking about the viewing and then accompanying the person to see the body. In this way future guilt – 'I wish I had seen her' – can be avoided. The viewing can be a time for silent prayer and weeping, and this may be more appropriate a day or so before the funeral rather than immediately before the service.

Some people will feel no desire to view the body,

preferring to remember the deceased as he was. For these people, viewing the body would not be so much unhelpful as irrelevant. I have met very few people who have regretted seeing the body of a loved one after death; I have met many more who regretted not seeing their loved one.

The funeral service

The clergyman or minister will advise on the number of services and the appropriate venues for these services. Customs vary in different cultures. In some areas it is still fitting to have a service in the home of the deceased, followed by a short committal at the graveside or at the crematorium. In other areas, services are held in the funeral parlour where there is a small chapel. Often services will be held in a local church followed by the brief service of committal.

The minister will also advise on the singing and choice of hymns. While most ministers follow the same basic outline for a funeral service, they are usually only too willing to incorporate items that make the service unique and personal to the family that has been bereaved.

A word for ministers

Occasionally the complaint is heard after a funeral service, 'It was so impersonal, not even her name was mentioned.' When taking a funeral service we have to steer a difficult course between formality and informality. The formal structure and wording of the service will be a safe stronghold for many grieving people; but the formality should not be cold and impersonal. Informality, on the other hand, can be comforting, providing it does not degenerate into sentimentality or detract from the solemnity and dignity of the occasion. It is important for the relatives that in the funeral service the unique personality and life of the deceased is recognized. What may be another funeral for us may be a new and traumatic event for the family.

Usually the minister will visit the family both before and after the funeral. The first visit allows us to develop some rapport with the family, especially if they were previously unknown to us. This visit gives us the opportunity to do some homework, discovering something about the deceased and the family situation so that we can speak a relevant word into the situation.

Many families are nervous about the funeral service. What will happen? What must they do? Where will they sit? During the first visit we can talk about the service, its purpose and contents, so that the family knows and understands what is going to happen. It can be helpful to alert the family to some of the more traumatic moments, such as the first sight of the coffin, and the 'disappearance' of the coffin at the crematorium.

A leaflet containing a few relevant scripture portions and a prayer can be left with the family. Such leaflets can be obtained from the Bible Society and Christian Publicity Organization (addresses are in the appendix, under 'comfort for the bereaved'). I have sometimes typed a prayer for a person, suggesting that it be used at night or in the morning. The following prayer[2] could be used or modified (substituting 'she' or 'her' as appropriate):

Uplift my grief

Grant, O Lord, that I may keep in loving remembrance him who has gone before, him who has stood by me and helped me, whose love and fellowship have given me so many years of happiness.

May I hold my head high and live my span of life with honour, integrity and full enjoyment.

Uplift my grief in losing him into Thy kingdom, lest it sour my relationship with others and the life I have ahead of me.

Help me not to give way to self-pity in my loneliness, but to people it with others so that, without disloyalty to the memory of my beloved, my life may blosson again like a rose.

Help me always to remember that life itself is a gift from Thee to be lived to the full in company with others.

Deepen my conviction that death is but a gentle step from darkness to light.
Amen.

Purposes of the funeral service

Although funeral services will vary within different cultures and within different denominations, the main purposes of such services remain the same.

A time to say farewell

The funeral is an important affirmation of the fact of death, unwelcome and painful though it may be. The public nature of funeral services is significant. The private acceptance of death can become more real at the public funeral. Failure to attend the funeral could lead to grief remaining locked within an individual. The public acknowledgment of death at a funeral strengthens the individual's acceptance of death's reality. The funeral is the one public ritual left in our death-denying society. For some people death is not faced and tears do not flow until the funeral when the public farewell is made. The funeral provides the first step in bereavement for certain individuals. This is a step towards healing, a step that should not be avoided.

A time to give thanks

Some part of the funeral service should be focused on the person who has died. Empty, dishonest eulogies should have no place. Genuine tributes have an important place. A unique life has ended and thanksgiving is appropriate. Ministers will need to do their homework if this part of the service, a vital part for the relatives, is to be meaningful. The life of the deceased should be placed within the context of the goodness and faithfulness of God. Where there has been a living and personal faith in Jesus Christ, the fragrance of the knowledge of Christ will permeate the service.

A time to renew faith

While, as Christians, we accept the reality of death, we deny its finality. We have an Easter faith centred on an empty tomb, not an occupied cross. We grieve when our loved ones die, but our grief is without despair. The shadow of death is bright with hope. At the funeral service we affirm our belief in Jesus Christ risen from the dead, and the relevance of his resurrection to all believers: 'I am the resurrection and the life. He who believes in me will live, even though he dies . . .' (John 11:25). We affirm our conviction that death is not a terminus but a thoroughfare that leads to life with Christ: 'I will come back and take you to be with me that you also may be where I am' (John 14:3). We renew our faith in the sovereign control of God who makes no mistakes working out his plans, and from whom nothing will ever separate the believer (Rom 8:28,38,39). We open our hearts to the special grace of the God of all comfort (2 Cor 1:3,4).

The resurrection faith of the Christian can be powerfully expressed at the funeral by the singing of hymns. Hymns that focus on the person and work of Jesus Christ have an objectivity that many will find helpful. Hymns that emphasize the resurrection theme can both express and challenge faith. However, where the group attending the funeral is expected to be small or is unaccustomed to singing, the reading of a hymn may be more appropriate.

When he was dying the evangelist D L Moody is reported to have made this statement: 'Soon you will read in the newspapers that Moody is dead. Don't you believe it, for I shall be more alive than I am now.' More alive than now: that is the Christian hope we celebrate at a funeral.

A celebration at every funeral?

'What about my husband/wife who has made no profession of faith in Jesus Christ?' There are few questions that so torment the mind as this one. It is an agonizing and unanswerable question. We do not know exactly what is each individual's standing before God. Only God knows that. We often make faith a much more intellectual and complicated exercise than is warranted by the New Testament teaching, with its emphasis on the childlike simplicity of faith. We do not know what inner working of God's Spirit may have taken place in a person's life as they approached death. What we *do* know is that God's justice far exceeds human justice and God's love is 'broader than the measures of man's mind'. It is to our God who is all-fair and all-loving that we commit those in whom we have seen no evidence of faith. Such a commitment is a massive step of faith, which only those who have to make it will understand.

Burial or cremation?

The Bible offers no clear guidance on the question of burial or cremation. Neither method was used in Bible times. Cremation was not a Jewish practice, and burial places tended to be caves. As is often the case, the Bible is 'more concerned with motives rather than methods when it comes to the question of the disposal of the dead'.[3]

The body is God's creation and as such should be treated with respect and dignity. The body is not basically evil, and man is more than 'an angel in a slot machine'. Just as Jesus' body was treated with respect by his friends, so our funeral services are an acknowledgment of our respect for the body and the unique individual whose life was expressed through that body. In each situation, a decision must be made about the most dignified and practical way of disposing of the body. It is helpful if people have made their feelings known on this issue beforehand. Indeed it is a comfort to relatives when they know that in the details of the funeral, the wishes of the deceased are being carried out.

If it is decided to have a service of cremation, the funeral director, when arranging the service, may ask the family about the disposal of the ashes. Most families agree to the ashes being dispersed by the crematorium officials in the grounds of the crematorium. Alternatively, if requested, a small amount of the ash may be given to the family. One family asked that the ashes be given to them so that they might dispose of them. Some of the ash was scattered around the grave of another member of the family; the minister was present and led in a brief prayer. The remainder of the ash was scattered in the family garden and a rose bush was planted in memory of the deceased.

Signpost to tomorrow

There is no need to dread the funeral. Surrounded and supported by the presence and prayers of God's people, the bereaved are wonderfully upheld. Those who are responsible for the funeral can be trusted. It is not a new or frightening experience for the funeral director or the minister. At the funeral, the bereaved take the first significant step along the road of grief. Although the road is long and hard, it is the road to healing. The funeral is the signpost to God's tomorrow.

8
The long road

Christians must grieve. We should beware of the attitude which says, 'My loved one is in heaven, why should I be sad?' That the loved one is with the Lord gives cause for joy and hope; that the loved one is away from us is a reason for sadness and grief. When Paul wrote to the Thessalonians, he did not instruct them to refrain from grief. He assured them that the despair, so often an ingredient of grief, had been destroyed by the gospel of the risen Christ: 'Brothers we do not want you . . . to grieve like the rest of men, who have no hope' (1 Thess 4:13). It is the nature rather than the fact of grief that is changed by the gospel. Hope in the living Christ who has conquered death, adds a new dimension to grief, but some of the pain of grief remains. 'Religious beliefs are not a substitute for grief: they should be a vehicle for its healthy expression.'[1]

The beliefs we hold dear as Christians – the sovereignty and love of God, the resurrection of Christ and the hope of heaven – will all be tested along the road of bereavement. It is a long, winding road with many dark patches. The shadow of death will often feel dark and low. Nevertheless, these truths, after the testing, will add a lustre to the shadow and a new depth to our Christian experience. We never know how much we really believe anything until its truth or falsehood is put under fire. The assault of grief may cause us to question the very basics of our faith. The questioning may be agonizing, even at times violent. But, like many before us, we will discover that pain tempers conviction. After testing we 'shall come forth as gold' (Job 23:10).

Grief is inevitable

If we love, we will grieve; for grief is the other side of the coin of love. We cannot love without taking the risk of losing the one we love and plunging into grief. The only way to avoid grief is to avoid love. But to avoid love, for fear of facing grief, involves a far greater risk, as C S Lewis observes with chilling logic:

> To love at all is to be vulnerable. Love anything and your heart will certainly be wrung and possibly broken. If you want to make sure of keeping it intact, you must give your heart to no one, not even to an animal. Wrap it carefully around with hobbies and little luxuries; avoid all entanglements; lock it up safe in the casket or coffin of your selfishness. But in that casket – safe, dark, motionless, airless – it will change. It will not be broken; it will become unbreakable, impenetrable, irredeemable . . .[2]

There is a cost to pay for loving, but there is a greater cost to pay for refusing to love.

Grief is essential

Those who refuse to grieve, or are unable to grieve in an appropriate way, will find it much more difficult, if not impossible, to come to terms with their bereavement. The acceptance of death and the discovery of a new life lie along the pathway of grief. The pain of grief must be experienced in all its depth and length. Only then will it recede. There is no easy escape route from the painful reality of bereavement. The long road must be travelled. The grief-work must be accomplished if healing is to come. Colin Murray Parkes, in his authoritative work on grief in adult life, states candidly, 'The bereaved person has a painful and difficult task to perform which cannot be avoided and cannot be rushed.'[3]

Signposts along the road

When you are travelling along a totally unfamiliar road, it is encouraging now and again to come across a signpost that both assures you that you are on the right road and points you in the right direction. If the lonely road of bereavement is new for you, here are some signposts. But first, a word of warning! Don't expect to progress systematically from one post to the next. The experience of bereavement is not like that. You will see the same signpost and the same scenery many times along this road. C S Lewis has summed up the 'grieving process':

> Grief is like a long valley, a winding valley where any bend may reveal a totally new landscape. [But] not every bend does. Sometimes the surprise is the opposite one; you are presented with exactly the same sort of country you thought you had left behind miles ago. That is when you wonder whether the valley isn't a circular trench. But it isn't. There are partial recurrences, but the sequence doesn't repeat.[4]

Four stages in the experience of grief have been identified: numbness, pining, depression and recovery.[5] Although the expression and duration of these stages varies from person to person, there is a traceable pattern to grief.

Numbness

This, the first stage of grief, may last from a few minutes to a few days, extending occasionally to a few weeks. It assumes different and apparently opposite forms. For some people, this numbness or shock immediately after a death causes them to become hyperactive. They rush around arranging the funeral and disposing of the deceased person's belongings. In all this intense activity there is no sign of tears and no display of sadness. In contrast, other people, especially after a sudden death, are stunned, the emotions and the will seemingly paralysed. Again, little or no reaction is shown to the death. In the cases of these people, their families and friends need to assume responsibility for almost everything, from the funeral arrangements to the household chores. Gradually pangs of grief pierce the blanket of shock, allowing the pain of grief to infiltrate. The anaesthetic of shock has worn off and now the pain must be borne.

Pining

This stage can last for several weeks and even months. The bereaved is preoccupied with thoughts of the dead person. The events leading up to the death are recalled and repeated many times. Now it is easier to cry and the crying will be frequent and deep. This is normal. All sorts of unexpected 'triggers' will start off the crying. It may be a comment from a visitor, a scene on the television, the discovery of something belonging to the person who has died or the prayer of a Christian friend. Hymns can act as triggers for grief. The bereaved suddenly begin to notice the vast number of references to death and heaven there are in our hymns.

At this stage, the bereaved are restless, moving from one task to another without doing any of them properly because concentration is so hard. Feelings of fear and panic can be alarmingly real at this time – 'How am I going to cope?' There may also be some distressing physical symptoms, loss of appetite, palpitations and indigestion – 'The whole thing has hit my stomach.'

As the months following the death pass, this acute pain of grief recedes. That is to say, the acute pain is not felt all the time as in the early weeks. However, when the pain returns, as it often does, it returns with a new ferocity that can be frightening. The periods of acute pain get less, but when they come they can be more intense. These pangs of grief, these 'hot pokers', can recur years after the bereavement.

It is important, if possible, not to make any major decision like moving house and forming new and permanent relationships during the first two stages of grief. These should be delayed until the mind is more settled and rational, because at these stages the bereaved are very vulnerable. The pain of grief cannot be escaped by moving to another house where there are no memories. Memories lodge more firmly in the mind than in a building. To move away from familiar surroundings is in fact to bring about a second bereavement: not only has a loved one been lost but so have familiar friends and scenes. The greater the loss, the greater the challenge of adjustment.

Depression

Replacing the stage of pining, or acute grief, is depression. The sharp pain of earlier days has now become a dull ache. At this time, the bereaved person can lose confidence and withdraw from people. Small routine tasks seem mountainous. The widow may feel that there is now no point in cooking meals since she is on her own. She looks at the world through dark glasses; everything appears dull.

Many bereaved people are conscious of having two faces, or wearing two masks, a public one and a private one. In public they appear to be coping, so much so that people remark how well they are 'getting over it'. How that hurts! If only people knew! They do not see the private tears, nor do they feel the emptiness of the house at night when the doors are bolted and all is so quiet and dark. They do not understand how long an evening alone can be. On the surface, to have a public and a private face smacks of hypocrisy. But in this instance that is not so. It is in fact a sign of moving forward along the road of grief. The bereaved has the courage to be 'normal' in public. Slowly progress is being made.

Recovery

In one sense, there is no complete recovery from deep bereavement, no end to the long road. The person who has died will always be missed. We should beware of concluding that because we will miss our loved one or friend so deeply, we are not recovering from bereavement. What matters is not reaching the end of the long road but moving along it. If we keep moving along the road, we are recovering. Progress will sometimes be slow and there will be much dogged plodding and uphill trudging.

C S Lewis paints a graphic picture of what it means to 'get over' bereavement. He draws a comparison with losing a limb. For the man who has had his leg amputated, part of him is missing and will always be missing, even if he gets a wooden leg and learns to walk again. People will say he's 'got over it'.

> But he will probably have recurrent pains in the stump all his life, and perhaps pretty bad ones; and he will always be a one-legged man. There will be hardly any moment when he forgets it. Bathing, dressing, sitting down and getting up again, even lying in bed, will all be different. His whole way of life will be changed. All sorts of pleasures and activities that he once took for granted will have to be simply written off.[6]

Recovering from bereavement is all about learning to live with the loss and adjusting to the new way of life.

As with so many issues in life, God's will lies not in the removal of the problem, but in living with it, strengthened by his grace. God makes the changes, not so much in our circumstances, as in ourselves.

New relationships

To recover from bereavement means to reach a point when the pain of grief has receded sufficiently to allow a person to build new relationships and to plan a new future. There is an understandable reluctance, if not guilt, at the prospect of forming new friendships and making new plans for the future. The bereaved can feel a gnawing sense of disloyalty towards the person who has died. This feeling of guilt can be eased by the thought that the loved one who has died would want the one who is left to live again and to discover a new life. Such a discovery need not entail disloyalty.

After the death of her husband, Ingrid Trobisch felt that she would not want to love a man again because she could not stand the pain of losing him. With characteristic honesty she writes: 'It was so much more comfortable to lock up my feelings and not risk being hurt.' Many a widow or widower will have no difficulty identifying with that sentiment. But gradually Ingrid Trobisch made a discovery: 'I learned that we don't honour the dead by dying with them. We honour them by being God's servants and stewards, by living for him and for others.'[7]

Forming new relationships takes time. A new relationship that leads to marriage should not be an attempt to replace the lost one, but rather an expression of renewed confidence that life is still worth living and meaningful relationships are still possible. It is more helpful to think of marriages after bereavement as new marriages rather than remarriages.

A new marriage may be part of God's plan. Ingrid Trobisch counsels wisely on this matter: 'What God desires, he must also inspire. He gives only the best to those who leave the choice with him. It is wrong to push open a door that God has closed.'[8]

Recovering from bereavement does not involve forgetting the one who has died. That person can never be forgotten. Recovery means not forgetfulness but remembering with greater courage.

Some people reach the stage of recovery after six months; two years is a more common period of time. It would be wrong to be dogmatic about the duration of these stages of grief. Each individual walks his or her own pathway. Some walk more quickly than others; some have more help than others.

9
Help along the road

Bishop John V Taylor tells the moving story of someone who helped in a time of bereavement. A West Indian woman was told of her husband's death in a street accident. Stunned by the news, she sat motionless, speechless, totally unresponsive. She was like someone in a trance. No one could communicate with her. Then one of her children's school teachers arrived:

> Without a word she threw an arm around the tight shoulders, clasping them with her full strength. The white cheek was thrust hard against the brown. Then as the unrelenting pain seeped through to her the newcomer's tears began to flow, falling on their two hands linked in the woman's lap. For a long time that is all that was happening. Then at last the West Indian woman started to sob. Still not a word was spoken and after a while the visitor got up and went, leaving her contribution to help the family meet its immediate needs.[1]

The helper

'I want to help but I don't know what to say.' Why do we so often assume that helping means saying something? It is our presence with the bereaved and our attitude towards them that matter most. Our empathy – feeling their feelings – rather than our sympathy ('I feel so sorry for you') is what will bring greatest comfort. The teacher visiting the West Indian woman said nothing but accomplished much. It is this capacity to feel the pain of another, this willingness to take on board the sorrow and shock that another person is experiencing, that Paul has in mind when he urges believers to 'mourn with those who mourn' (Rom 12:15).

'I feel so helpless'

The bereaved often feel a sense of helplessness that can be shared by the helper. Colin Murray Parkes analyses the pain of helplessness that is felt when trying to comfort the bereaved:

> It stems from the awareness of both parties that neither can give the other what he wants. The helper cannot bring back the person who is dead and the bereaved person cannot gratify the helper by seeming helped. No wonder that both parties feel dissatisfied with the encounter.[2]

In helping the bereaved we must come to terms with our own feelings of helplessness. The grieving person will find a comfort in our honest helplessness that will never be found in slick, irrelevant platitudes. There is a strange but real fellowship in shared helplessness.

Let us therefore accept the feeling of helplessness as God's gift, and allow him to use it to draw us close to the bereaved. Far from disqualifying us from helping, helplessness is one of the first requirements of a helper.

Letters of sympathy

Cards and letters can bring comfort, not only in the

early days of bereavement but in later weeks when the thoughts expressed in them can be appreciated more deeply. A letter can be one way of affirming the worth of the person who has died. Such a letter, sensitively written, reminds the bereaved that there are those who care and this eases the feelings of fear and insecurity.

A letter should be brief. Do not hesitate to mention the name of the person who has died, sharing something of what that person meant to you. One incident or conversation might be recalled. Any appreciation the deceased expressed to you of the person to whom you are writing can be appropriately shared. Such a sharing may ease any feelings of guilt or failure that the bereaved is experiencing. Do not be glib about assurances of prayer. Try to be specific about when and what you are praying. Ask God to give you one thought from scripture that you can share. Don't preach; don't try to explain what has happened. Be careful about saying that you know exactly how they feel; you don't! Every experience of bereavement is unique. Your task is not to share your experience of bereavement, but to share theirs.

It is sometimes more appropriate to write this kind of letter a few weeks after the death, at a time when you have begun to recover from the shock of the death and are better able to gather your thoughts about the deceased. Such a letter will also be more significant to the bereaved when they too have moved a little way down the long road. The most appropriate action immediately following the death may well be simply a card or a very brief note.

Anniversaries and birthdays are particularly poignant experiences for the bereaved. The first anniversary of the death is often a time when the detailed events of the death are re-lived and the strong pangs of early grief return for a while. The helper should seek to remember anniversaries and birthdays and provide the appropriate encouragement through a visit, a card, a letter or some flowers. In this way you, the helper, provide a tangible reminder that you have not forgotten that the road of bereavement is a long one.

'I don't want to upset her'

Letters and cards can upset the bereaved, causing tears to flow as the reality of what has happened dawns more clearly with each expression of sympathy. There is the understandable temptation to want to shield the bereaved from this pain and so to keep the cards and letters from them. Such misguided love fails to recognize the importance of normal grieving – tears must flow. If letters and cards assist in the early expression of grief, they have fulfilled a valuable task, a healing task.

I recall a woman whose husband died very suddenly. The shock of his death so stunned his widow that she found it very hard to feel or express any sorrow. The problem was compounded by well-meaning relatives who 'took over' the widow, removing her from her home, protecting her from visitors, shielding her from letters and cards and insisting that she did not attend her husband's funeral. The result of this over-protective love was that the widow became locked in a cell of shock. She was not set free to grieve. It was many years before she was able to return to church. The long road of grief was made even longer by a loving family who didn't want their mother to be upset.

Acceptance

The bereaved sometimes find that people ignore them and even go out of their way to avoid them. Those who do this are not being deliberately unkind. They are embarrassed and do not know either how to handle the death or what to say to the bereaved. It is not unusual for the bereaved to find themselves having to comfort the very friends who should be comforting them.

The helper needs to accept the bereaved as they are, with all the mixed emotions that accompany grief. When the bereaved are numb with shock, the helper should wait patiently and quietly without trying to force a response. Silences need not be embarrassing.

Tears must be accepted. The helper should not feel duty-bound to be 'strong' and keep his feelings under control. The strong Son of God wept with Mary and Martha following the death of Lazarus. There is nothing weak or unmanly about tears.

Expressions of anger, so common during bereavement, should also be accepted by the helper who should refrain from making judgmental statements or taking the angry outburst personally. Much more is said about this subject in chapter twelve.

Give sorrow words

Let the bereaved speak when they are ready. Allow them, especially in the early days of their grief, to speak repeatedly about the events leading up to the death. Be willing, as the helper, to encourage talking by gentle, sensitive questions and to listen to the same story repeated many times. Talking is the beginning of the grieving process, the first step towards healing. It is important for the bereaved to give sorrow words, even though the words might at times be violent or alarming.

Thoughts of suicide

The helper should not be shocked if the bereaved makes a statement which sounds suicidal. 'I wouldn't care if I died tomorrow' is an expression of loneliness and despair and does not necessarily contain a suicidal intention.

We are often afraid of mentioning suicide lest, by doing so, we plant the idea in a person's mind. If a person is thinking about suicide, having reached the depths of despair, it is better for that person to be able to talk about his thoughts than to keep them to himself. If a person is not really thinking about suicide, it is highly unlikely that the mention of it by the helper will sow a seed in his mind. Murray Parkes suggests that . . . 'A simple question, "Has it been so bad that you have thought of killing yourself?" is more likely to save a life than take one.'[3]

Reassurance

The bereaved often suffer a loss of self-confidence which the helper can do much to restore, although the restoration may take many months. The widow wonders how she will cope with all the responsibilities previously handled by her husband. The worlds of banking and building societies, solicitors and estate agents, car maintenance and do-it-yourself, may be alien, frightening worlds. The widower, likewise, suffers a loss of self-confidence. His wife may have paid all the bills and made the kitchen her domain. He now has to enter the strange world of the supermarket. This he does with difficulty, trying to find where everything is, and with pain, noticing how many couples are shopping together.

The helper can enter these new worlds with the bereaved. It is important to do things with the bereaved rather than for them. The helper's aim should be to lead the bereaved towards an acceptance of new responsibilities. Hence sharing new responsibilities with them rather than taking responsibility from them is the way to lead them into the new future. Many widowers have been greatly helped by a friend who has written down some basic cooking instructions for them. The widow may appreciate the help of a man in the church who has expertise in finance, providing he is discreet and able to keep a confidence.

The bereaved feel that death has altered their status. The wife whose husband has died is now labelled a 'widow' by society. Who is she? She is no longer married, but she does not feel or want to feel single. She wonders now whether she can invite to *her* home the friends she and her husband used to invite to *their* home. Death has not only broken one relationship, it has altered many others. To the bereaved, there appear to be so many activities that couples do together socially that cannot be done by the widow or widower. In the church, groups consisting predominantly of couples make the widow and widower (and the single person) feel isolated and unwanted.

Danger

A bereaved person is extremely vulnerable. The needs of the bereaved for comfort, companionship and love, both emotional and physical, are strong. The helper should be keenly aware of this vulnerability, being careful not to take advantage of it. The dangers of men counselling widows or women counselling widowers are obvious, as they are in any counselling situation. What begins with a desire to comfort can easily develop into the kind of relationship in which the bereavement needs are not in fact met. The relationship as it develops becomes a substitute for bereavement or an escape from the pain of grief. When such a relationship develops, the grief-work is not completed; it is discarded in favour of the new relationship. Such a friendship may be a welcome relief from the heavy monotony of grief, but it is a diversion into a cul-de-sac. The main road, the long road of bereavement, must be joined again at some point. No relationship, however deep, can be a substitute for grieving.

'Am I going crazy?'

Some of the emotions associated with grief are so intense that many bereaved people need reassuring that their reactions are perfectly normal. 'I thought I was going off my head' is the kind of comment often heard during the stage of acute grief. Vivid dreams about the deceased, talking to them and sensing their presence are all normal symptoms of grief. Some of these emotions are so new and so strong that the bereaved person might question his or her sanity. However, there is no reason to regard any of these as signs of mental illness.[4] Most people cope with the experience of grief, and only a very small number will need special help.

There are two signs to look for which might indicate abnormal grief and suggest that special help is needed. The first is the total absence of emotion, the characteristic of the first stage of grief, continuing for several weeks or months. If after this longer period there have been no tears, no sadness, no talking about the dead person, it might be advisable to consult a doctor. The second sign is the prolonging, well past the 'normal' time, of any of the intense expressions of grief, like anger or guilt.

Guilt

Along with anger, guilt and remorse are the strongest pains experienced by those in bereavement. The helper may feel that much of the guilt is false, unjustified, lacking real foundation. It is nevertheless, painfully real, even if it is distorted. The bereaved may feel guilty about not having loved the deceased enough, or about having wanted the patient to die quickly. The helper must listen carefully and patiently as the bereaved speaks of his guilt, letting him talk through the guilt. Do not rush to lightly dismiss it. Where the guilt is grounded in fact, where there has been real failure on the part of the bereaved, God's forgiveness can be asked for and claimed on the basis of Christ's finished work on the cross. God, our heavenly Father, can also be sought for the healing of memories, once the sin is forgiven. Guilt that is neither talked about nor forgiven will prolong and distort bereavement. Unexpressed and unresolved guilt is responsible for much of the pain and delay in 'recovery' from bereavement.

Friendship

It often happens that a bereaved person is surrounded by family and friends who give much help during the early days of grief. Then after a few days or weeks much of that support is withdrawn as the 'helpers' return to their daily routines, leaving the bereaved to discover new routines. It is precisely at this time that practical help is needed. By certain simple commitments the helper can assist the bereaved to make some vital adjustments to his way of life. A phone call each morning, a trip to the supermarket each Thursday afternoon, a visit to the bereaved at a set time every fortnight are all practical ways of helping the bereaved towards establishing a new pattern of life.

The helper should also be aware of the special value of little surprises for the bereaved, like the unexpected visit, the bunch of flowers from the church, a day out in the car, a visit to the theatre. Weekends can be especially lonely. It seems to the bereaved that everyone else is with their families, while they are alone. In our churches those with the gift of hospitality should be encouraged to use it for the benefit of the lonely, the elderly and the bereaved, especially at weekends. As Christians we need to grasp the concept of the extended family and teach our children to grasp it also, so that having people to lunch or for coffee after the Sunday service becomes the norm rather than the exception.

The helper should be sensitive to the ordeal of coping with the 'firsts'. The list of 'firsts' ranges from returning home, going to the familiar shops, going away on holiday and returning to church. Whenever something is tackled for the first time after a bereavement a step forward along the road of grief is taken. Some of these 'firsts' can be tackled alone, others in company. Bereaved people find the party and the social event particularly hard experiences to face. The happiness and joviality of such events conflict with the deep inner sadness of their present experience. The helper should be alert to this difficulty and understand the reluctance of the bereaved to attend such functions.

Above all, friendship with the bereaved needs to be sustained over a long period of time. The observation of so many who have travelled the long road of bereavement is that very few walk the whole distance with them. It seems to the bereaved that everybody else recovers from their bereavement so much more quickly than they do themselves. It cannot be over-stressed that the grieving process is a long one and the helper must be prepared for a lengthy ministry.

Bereavement recovery groups

During bereavement, some people, especially those who lack strong family support, appreciate the company of others who are also trying to cope with grief. On a road that is new and long, it can be reassuring to have the friendship of fellow travellers. 'Cruse' – the National Organization for the Widowed and their Children – offers a counselling service for the bereaved, and through its branches in different parts of the country provides opportunities for social contact with other bereaved people. Through such groups, the bereaved are able to meet with those who can identify with their feelings; they can begin to build new relationships; they can receive encouragement in building a new life; they can also feel that they are giving help to fellow pilgrims. The address of 'Cruse' and other organizations that offer support to the bereaved are listed in the appendix.

Some local churches have formed groups to help the bereaved. The group help is especially relevant during the first year of bereavement. It is important that such groups are led by those with insight into the experience of grief. If this insight has been received along the road of personal experience, it is important that these leaders have progressed a considerable way along that road and experienced 'recovery'. The group might meet once a month. Although it will not meet the needs of every bereaved person, the mutual sharing of feelings by the group and the practical encouraging of one another will prove of value to some. Such a group will have a limited ministry for a limited time. People should be encouraged to leave such a group so that it does not become a permanent prop. The decision to leave the group should be seen as a positive step forward.

The local church might also consider training a few people as bereavement counsellors. The minister or pastor would then be able to link bereaved families and individuals to someone in the church who could visit the home after the funeral and seek to build an ongoing relationship. The counsellors could meet together to encourage one another, being careful not to betray confidences entrusted to them.

As individual Christians and church communities, we have much to offer the bereaved. Most bereaved people need a helper. Is this God's calling to you?

10
The loss of a child

'I had lost part of my own body. I had lost my future, for my only child had died. I had lost my identity. Was I a mother any more?' These were the feelings of a mother after her twelve year old daughter had died. The loss of a child is surely the most distressing and long-lasting of all griefs. This is particularly so today in a society where the death of a child is comparatively rare.

All the normal reactions of bereavement are present in a more intense form following the death of a child. This bereavement road is a very long one. King David expressed his grief at the death of his son Absalom, who was a young man rather than a child. His grief will be understood by many a parent whose son or daughter has died: 'The king was shaken. He went up to the room over the gateway and wept. As he went, he said: "O my son Absalom! My son, my son Absalom! If only I had died instead of you – O Absalom, my son, my son!" ' (2 Sam 18:33). All the agony of a parent's grief is there, together with the eager but futile willingness to change places with his son.

The intensity of grief following the death of a child will not be understood by those outside the family if the value of a life is assessed in terms of years and achievements. It is not the number of accomplishments that matter, but rather ' . . . the nature of the relationship and the meaning of the lost member to the survivors that is significant'.[1] The bond between parents and a child is unique. The death of a child therefore leaves an emptiness that may last a lifetime.

So hard to accept

The death of a child, whether suddenly by accident or after a long illness, is unfair. It feels wrong, offending our innate sense of justice. It seems cruel. So much unfulfilled potential! The death of a child leaves the family devastated. It is so impossible to understand and so difficult to accept. Some would say: 'No reason is sufficient to explain the death of a child. There is no justice or justification in a child's death.'[2]

Parents will have painful reminders of their child and they will face experiences that are strange and new. Some parents experience the same symptoms that their child had during the last illness. It is not uncommon for a parent to 'see' his child among a group of children. Then the pangs of grief hurt all the more with the realization that the child, so like his own, is someone else. Small incidents, like hearing a child cry or watching a group of children at play, will trigger the overflow of grief. As in all grief, tears are normal and necessary, a vital part of healing. Never apologize for tears. Experiencing the same symptoms, 'seeing' the child and weeping uncontrollably are all normal and proper expressions of grief.

As with all bereavements, anniversaries are particularly poignant moments. Many parents, years after the death of their child, know how old that child would have been on each birthday. Seeing your child's friends and contemporaries grow up, change schools, go to work, get married, have families, are all reminders to you of what might have been.

The need to talk

One of the greatest needs of parents who have lost a child is to talk – about the child, the past, the events leading up to the death, and especially their own feelings. Some parents, and fathers in particular, may find it very difficult to talk. It may be weeks or months before a father can talk about his child and his own feelings. It may be helpful for parents to make a pact, painful though it will be, that they will talk about the child. This idea of making such an agreement is suggested by one writer who made a pact with her husband following the death of their ten year old son. She writes: 'To avoid remembering him, to avoid discussing him, recalling his likes and dislikes, his character, his humour, seemed like letting him die twice. And this we simply would not do.'[3]

Visitors entering a home after the death of a child need to provide an atmosphere in which the family, including the children, can feel free to express their sadness, their disappointment and their bewilderment and, not least, their anger. Visitors should not avoid mentioning the name of the child. Parents and children need to talk about the boy or girl who will always be so precious to them.

Company and solitude

Grieving parents need both company and solitude, and it is not easy to get the balance right. Immediately following the death and the funeral, there can be so many people around that the grieving parents long for privacy. For some, tears will only flow in the solitary place. God inhabits that place, and many meet him there in a deeply personal way.

At times of deep grief, we also need human support. The kind of person many find helpful is the one who comes in and takes gentle initiative, doing the washing-up or taking away the washing and bringing it back the next day. The grieving mother finds it difficult to cope with the well-meaning friend or relative who fusses, asking constantly what they can do next. The invitation to 'Call me if you need help' will rarely be taken up, for the grieving mother lacks the will to accept the offer. In grief, the mind is confused and numb, unable to make decisions or take initiatives. Others, for a while at least, must take these initiatives and keep the family functioning.

Marriage under stress

The death of a child puts a strain on the parents' relationship. On the face of it you might expect that two people who had experienced the death of their child would be drawn closer than ever to one another. It does not always work out that way. As Harriet Sarnoff Schiff observes: 'Common grief is not the best possible adhesive to cement a marriage.'[4] Why not? Although couples can, to some extent, comfort one another, there is something about grief that is unique to each person. Even the individuals within a marriage relationship may grieve in different ways. Couples should therefore mourn as individuals as well as a couple. It may come as a shock to parents to discover that at times they are unable to help and comfort one another. This should not surprise them or worry them unduly. For 'you cannot lean on something bent double from its own burden'.[5] There are times, therefore, when parents may need separate counselling through bereavement.

Don't say . . .

When we are confronted by mystery, most of us feel compelled to say something. Simon Peter was never lost for words. He had a word for every occasion – unfortunately! On the mount of transfiguration, when Jesus appeared clothed in glory with Moses and Elijah, Peter, not knowing what to say, came up with plans for a building programme (Mark 9: 5,6)! For us to find ourselves lost for words is not failure, it is human and very often the most appropriate response. A silent hug speaks to the heart, trite words only wound.

'Time is a great healer,' we say. 'I don't want to be healed,' is the silent rebuke of the broken-hearted mother. 'Your burden is now lifted,' was the insensitively timed comment made to a mother whose daughter, suffering from spina bifida, had just died. Her daughter, a burden? What an outrageous thought! 'You'll be able to help others so much more . . .' What a price to pay for helping others! Although there is truth in some of these comments we make at the time of death, that truth cannot be appreciated by someone so close to death. When we make such comments, we are trying to hurry people too quickly away from the fact of death. It is the timing of these comments, rather than their truth, which is to be questioned.

Why God, in his sovereignty, has permitted the death of this child is the ultimate question. It is a natural question to ask, and an impossible one to answer. The answers we often suggest are in fact the *by-products* of the death, not the answer to the ultimate question. It may well be that a mother whose child has died *is* able to draw alongside people whose lives and families have been shattered by death. That pastoral sensitivity is the sovereign by-product and not the divine reason for the child's death. That ultimate and divine reason will be revealed, if necessary, in heaven.

Stillbirth

A lady of seventy commented that her son would have been fifty years old on a certain day. He had been stillborn. A mother rarely forgets a stillborn baby. A stillbirth can cause as much grief as the death of an older child.

Memories help the process of mourning. That is why grieving over a stillborn child is so difficult; there is little to remember. It is important that the parents of a stillborn baby be given the opportunity to see and hold the baby. Although the initial reaction to such an idea may be negative, if the opportunity is given later the response may be different. Some hospitals take a polaroid photo of the baby and keep it with their records, so that, if the parents wish, they can see it later.

It is helpful if the baby is given a name and the name is used in later conversations. A stillbirth must be registered. While this is a difficult experience for the father, it is often the first step in grieving. The certificate must be handed to the funeral director and a funeral arranged. Since 1974 in England and Wales (1976 in Scotland) it has been possible for the Area Health Authority to take responsibility for the burial of the baby. This facility can be used if the parents so desire. Although such a course of action may ease the immediate distress of the parents, it is questionable whether the long-term effects are helpful. Parents may later regret not having said 'Goodbye' by means of a funeral.

The mother may experience intense anger or guilt following a stillbirth. She may blame herself, the doctors or God. She may also have fears about any future pregnancy. Her great need is to talk through these different emotions with someone who understands the intensity of feeling. It may not be helpful for well-meaning friends to remove all signs of the expected birth from the house before mother comes home. It could help the mother to go through the baby clothes and work through some of the pain of grieving.

Cot death

Every year hundreds of babies, about one in every five

hundred in this country, die suddenly and unexpectedly in their sleep. These deaths are referred to as cot deaths or 'sudden infant death syndrome'. This is a clinical condition, now accepted internationally as a natural registerable cause of death.

Parents whose baby dies in this way often feel guilty, blaming themselves for the death. Almost always that guilt is totally without foundation. There was nothing that could be done either to anticipate or prevent the death.

The feelings of guilt are fed by several factors. The absence of any satisfactory medical explanation is one of them. Scientific information about cot deaths can ease this awful feeling of guilt. Such information can be obtained from the Foundation for the Study of Infant Deaths (address in the appendix). The visit of the police and the subsequent coroner's enquiry also tend to make the parents feel guilty. Information about the necessity of these legal investigations will allay fears and ease guilt. Finally, the comments of friends can hurt. Parents whose baby has died in this way are obviously very sensitive to remarks that could possibly be construed as indicating guilt.

It is perfectly natural for a mother whose baby has died as a result of a cot death to feel frightened and anxious in relation to other children, especially a subsequent baby. The mother feels helpless and sees no logical reason why the tragedy should not recur. Some mothers speak of 'cot-watching' when a new baby is born. Only the patient and understanding support of friends will allay these fears. Parents need reassuring that sudden infant death syndrome is not hereditary.

In some hospitals respiration monitors are used to monitor the breathing movements of babies up to one year old. The monitor includes an alarm which goes off (after say twenty seconds) if the baby does not breathe. In some regions these monitors can be obtained for use at home. This service would be for babies considered to be 'at risk'; such babies would include those born into a family where a cot death had previously occurred. Information about the availability and use of respiration monitors can be provided by hospitals or the Health Visitor.

The question of having another baby is an important one and a personal one. Only when parents are able to view another baby as a separate, unique individual is it appropriate to go forward with another pregnancy. There are no replacement babies.

Faith hangs on

'Can I still trust God?' can be the painful question asked by parents whose child has died. Often God does not give reasons for his actions. He does not explain why a child had to be taken or a baby be stillborn. We have to learn to live with the silence of God when it comes to reasons. Like Simon Peter, we hear Jesus saying to us, 'You do not realise now what I am doing, but later you will understand' (John 13:7). The 'later' may not be in this life, but in that fuller life beyond death when 'the dark things shall be made plain'.

God who is silent on reasons is not silent on revelation. Job found that a new revelation of God was God's way of meeting him in his hour of need. Job had a score of questions for God which were never answered. God knew that Job's greatest need was not answers to questions but the living presence of God.

God will always make himself known to his distressed children, though he may not reveal the reasons for his sovereign actions. He often provides a simple handle for faith to grasp. Jesus' words, 'Let the little children come to me' (Luke 18:16), remind us of our Lord's love for children. He will hold them in life and in death so that they are safe for ever. For one bereaved mother, two lines from the hymn . . . 'In Heavenly Love Abiding' provided the handle for her faith:

My Saviour has my treasure
And I will walk with Him.

While God may be silent about his reasons for allowing the death of a child, he is nevertheless a sharing God, feeling our sorrows and hurts in his heart. Much comfort has been found in the statement, 'In all their distress he too was distressed' (Isaiah 63:9). For 'there is no place where earth's sorrows are more felt than up in heaven'.

Faith gives back

All of us who are parents need to remind ourselves that our children are not ours; they are on loan to us from God. There is a very real sense in which they are his, loved by him even more than by us. On the death of their child, many parents find it helpful to consciously give their child back to God. They find it easier to live with that positive attitude of surrender than the passive, 'Our child was taken by God'.

When a child dies, we are challenged to give that child back to God by faith. That faith may struggle and scream, doubt and despair. But faith gives back. As we do this, God will lovingly move us forward showing us how to visit the house of our memories often, without being imprisoned in it.

11
Too young to understand?

Some adults, recalling their childhood experience of bereavement, feel again the pain of silence. Why was there so much talking in whispers when Mum died? Why was I shunted out of the room when visitors came to see Dad? What did the minister mean when he patted me on the head and said I was to be brave? Such questions, though rarely expressed at the time, take root in a child's mind. The child can so easily be left out when there is a death in the family. As adults, we justify this policy of exclusion with, 'He's too young to understand.' We forget that a child must also grieve and feel part of the grieving family too.

Conspiracy of silence

When children are ignored at a time of family bereavement they become frightened and their fertile imaginations are fired. Was it their fault that Daddy died? Will Mum be able to cope with the family on her own? A conspiracy of silence by adults discourages children from asking these questions and expressing the fears lying behind them. Children then conclude that death is one of those unmentionable subjects as far as they are concerned, one for adult discussion only.

The long-term effects of excluding children from normal family grieving can be serious. If a child is prevented from talking about death, especially the death of someone close, a fear of death may be cultivated in the child's mind, causing serious problems in adult life. The way in which a child handles death, especially the death of a parent, can be of crucial importance in the development of the child's personality.

Sula Wolf, whose book *Children Under Stress* includes a chapter on bereavement, complains that in the face of death and bereavement 'the behaviour of the parents is dictated by their own inner needs rather than by a realistic appreciation of their children's feelings'[1]. That may sound like a harsh judgment, but it may contain an embarrassing degree of truth when examined. In order to avoid the danger of projecting adult reactions on to a child, we need to ask how a child feels when faced by a death in the family.

Different needs at different times

The toddler, under four years old, has little or no idea of space or time. He lives in the present. He is therefore unable to grasp the finality of death. When three year old Sarah was told of the death of a neighbour, her response was, 'I will ask Jesus to make him better.' For Sarah, death was an illness.

The toddler's greatest fear is that he will be abandoned. He therefore needs kisses and cuddles, food and play, far more than explanations in words.

Children between the ages of four and seven ask a never-ending stream of questions. Many of their questions about death and heaven relate to the body, and may sound macabre to the adult ear. 'What do you eat in heaven?' 'Will there be sweets and ice cream in heaven?' Mark, a self-conscious five year old, was concerned to discover whether there were celestial changing rooms. His grandma's reply that there would be no need for changing rooms since we might not be wearing clothes was none too helpful!

It is at this age that some children make a link

between death and punishment. Will I die if I am naughty? Did Daddy die because I was rude and caused a scene at the dinner table? Do people die because in an angry moment you 'wish they were dead'? It is important to dispel these fears by assuring children that they will not die because they are naughty, and people do not die because of a wish. Incidentally, parents should guard against the impulsive remark, 'You'll be the death of me.' Such a comment, whether spoken lightly or in the heat of the moment by an adult, may be taken seriously and stored by a child.

If the parent has died following an illness, the child may well forge a link between illness and death. He will then become over-anxious about any illness, however minor, he or another member of the family develops. Following the death of one parent, a child may show extreme signs of anxiety if the other parent becomes ill: he may refuse to leave the house or become extremely attached to the sick parent. Children need to be reassured that people usually recover from illness, and that hospitals are places where people get better.

It is often at night that fears relating to death play on a child's mind. A six year old, informed that her mother 'died in her sleep', announced that she was never going to sleep again. Some children are frightened that the parent's ghost will come and haunt them. Windows therefore have to be shut and curtains drawn, and a light left on inside or outside the room. Nightmares and bed wetting can also be related to these fears.

It is at this age that children can be introduced helpfully and naturally to the basic idea of death through animals and pets. Beware of dishonesty when a pet dies. It is misguided love that protects the child from the death of the budgie, or the fact that the dog has been run over. Such events are important training experiences for children: they are learning the meaning of death. What is more, they are well able to handle these events.

Do not be surprised at how little emotion children of the four to seven age group show. The fear of being abandoned is still uppermost in their minds. It is stronger than sadness. What matters most is that the everyday needs of the child continue to be met, with as little alteration in the daily routine as possible.

How can we help children through bereavement? The answer may not sound very profound to the adult, but it is of supreme importance to the child: give constant love, reassurance and security. You will not fail a bereaved child if you supply these in wise abundance.

Between the ages of eight and eleven more adult responses to bereavement begin to appear. There may be tears and fits of sobbing. Children, especially from this age group upwards, need to cry. There is healing in tears. Crying is a God-given safety valve. Unfortunately our western culture has despised crying, regarding it as a symbol of weakness. Children therefore grow up being taught that 'big boys don't cry', and that crying is merely a way of drawing attention to ourselves. We must remember that Jesus wept in the face of death.

It is good to cry when we are sad. Research has shown a significant link between crying and talking. Children who cry most in bereavement also talk most about the deceased. Crying and talking are necessary ways of expressing grief and both should be encouraged. The father who refuses to talk to his child about the mother who has died, for fear of upsetting the child, is robbing the child and himself of healing tears and healing talk. It is important that tears are accepted as helpful and legitimate expressions of pain and sadness in the normal course of living. They will then be acceptable at times of bereavement.

After the death of a parent the child feels lost and alone. Matters that had been taken for granted are now questioned. Where will I go? Who will take care of me? The feelings of apprehension and despair behind these questions may be expressed in apathy towards simple routine functions such as eating, going to school and going to church. Though this apathy may be acute at first, it is usually a temporary symptom of bereavement which can be eased by gentle encouragement. The child's school teacher should be told of the bereavement, and allowance should be made for some change in academic performance, realizing that it is probably only temporary.

It is important to tell children the truth about the fact and the circumstances of death. They should not be told that Daddy has gone away to another country, since the finality of death is not conveyed by that picture. Tragic circumstances surrounding death, such as accident and suicide, should not be wholly hidden from children. The facts can be modified according to the age of the child and added to as he gets older. Honesty is important since the child will hear stories from his friends, the truth of which he must be able to check with the facts that he has been told. To lie to a child, for whatever motive, is to seriously undermine the child's faith in us. Furthermore we rarely get away with it, for a child has a built-in lie detector. Just as a child can handle facts better than silence, so he can handle the truth better than lies.

Great care should be taken over *how* a child is told of a parent's death, especially when setting the death within the context of God's purpose and God's love. In her book, *Children, Death and Bereavement*, Pat Wynnejones suggests the following guideline:

> There is a world of difference between saying 'God has taken Daddy,' as though that were the cause of death, and saying 'Daddy died of cancer – or in a car crash – but now God is taking care of him in heaven.' The former could destroy a child's faith in God's goodness – only a bad God would 'take' his Daddy, but the latter suggests that God is kind. He provides for us here on earth and up in heaven as well.[2]

Young people aged twelve upwards will show reactions similar to adults. They may have feelings of guilt or regret about their relationship with the deceased. They may blame either themselves or the surviving parent or the doctor for the death. It is helpful for some young people to remember a parent who has died by undertaking some of the tasks previously done by that parent. This is often an unconscious decision. After John's death, his sixteen year old daughter assumed some of the responsibilities in the family previously undertaken by John. Adopting one of the qualities in the parent they admired is a further positive way in which some young people express their grief. It may be helpful to ask the young person which part of their parent's character they would like to remember in this way.

Older children and young people may have questions about God's place in the family bereavement. Their childlike faith in a loving heavenly Father who provides for his children's needs will be tested. Let them ask their questions and express their doubts. Their faith will rise again, bruised but stronger as they learn that Christians are not immune from disaster and death and that in every crisis our loving God is still there, still caring, and still in control. The letters and cards, visits and practical help from friends can be pointed to as tokens of God's care.

Should children attend funerals?

Having recognized that children need to be included as much as possible in the family's grieving, we must attempt an answer to the question of children attending funerals. Again, we must look at this issue from the child's point of view. Seeing a child at a funeral may be harrowing for adults, but it is the need of the child that must be uppermost. A number of factors must be borne in mind. Children, especially those under nine, will be more affected by the expressions of grief from the adults they love, than by their own grief. How the surviving parent is going to cope with the funeral may be the key to deciding whether the child should attend.

A further consideration is that children need concrete evidence of death. The funeral provides that kind of evidence. Furthermore, the funeral conveys something of the finality of death which is a particularly difficult concept for a child to grasp.

If a child goes to a funeral service, he should be given some preparation so that he has some idea of what to expect. Children who do not attend the funeral service should be told something of what took place, so that they are not left guessing, usually wrongly. In this way the child can feel part of the grieving family.

God's love for the child

We will frequently be amazed by the resilience with which children face bereavement. This is a God-given resilience and a reflection of God's deep compassion for the bereaved child. The Bible speaks of God as the helper and defender of the fatherless (Ps 10:14,18), and one in whom the fatherless find compassion (Hos 14:3). God is a father to the fatherless (Ps 68:5). The Bible abounds with assurance of God's commitment to children without parents. How will these children experience the love of God?

Challenge to the church

God has left his people in no doubt that his commitment to the fatherless is to be channelled, in part, through their love. Practical concern for the orphan was, from earliest times, a strong feature of Israelite religion (Deut 24:17). When God called his people back to true faith, he included the command to 'defend the cause of the fatherless' (Isa 1:17). One of the features of Job's pastoral ministry was his rescuing the 'fatherless who had none to assist (them)' (Job 29:12).

The six year old boy whose father has died needs the companionship and counsel of a man. Children of this age model themselves on the parent of the same sex. It is therefore important that other people serve as models for identification for bereaved children. Sunday School teachers and others working with children in the life of the church should be particularly sensitive to their responsibility with regard to bereaved children. This responsibility exists not simply around the time of death, but during the years that follow.

To children of all ages, friendship needs to be offered at a variety of levels – school, leisure, future planning and Christian commitment. God has given to his church the responsibility of providing practical, ongoing support and encouragement to bereaved children. When we see a bereaved child in church, one phrase from the biblical definition of true religion should ring in our ears, 'to look after orphans . . . in their distress' (Jas 1:27).

12
Anger

'I eventually exploded and tore apart the baby's bedroom. Drawers were emptied, clothes flung far and wide, and the cot all but smashed. I screamed and scratched at the wallpaper. I felt utterly desperate and wanted to hurt everything and everybody that came within reach.' Such were the violent feelings of anger experienced by a mother whose baby boy had died within hours of birth.[1]

I recall my own struggle with anger at the time of John's death. One particular incident acted as a trigger. At John's request I went to ask the nurse for a painkiller; John's pain was rising and needed to be relieved quickly before it got a hold. The nurse was busy and irritated at being asked. She delayed coming with the pain relief for what seemed hours. As we waited, I felt anger welling up inside – anger I could not express to John for fear of adding to his agitation. Only later, outside the hospital, could I give vent to my feelings. I was surprised at the intensity and violence of the anger, out of all proportion to the particular incident.

Why was I so angry? I was angry because John was suffering so much. I was angry because I could not help him and I could not make the nurse act quickly. My anger had much to do with my own frustration and helplessness. Yet the anger had deeper roots. That incident with the nurse triggered off a deep-seated anger about the whole sordid business of a close friend dying of cancer. There was something so wrong and unfair about it. It was death, and the death of a friend, that made me so angry.

It is normal to get angry

Anger is all part of being human. In the face of suffering and death, it is normal to react with anger. The dying patient may well experience feelings of this kind which can be provoked by a variety of factors. Failure or delay in diagnosis can trigger anger: 'If only the doctor had taken me seriously when I first went to him.' The cold indiscriminate hand of death angers us. Why should such a young, dedicated servant of God have to die when his family needed him, a business career beckoned him and Christian service challenged him? John Hinton pinpoints a source of anger for some dying people who, having been accustomed to a self-controlled, orderly life, cannot come to terms with increasing weakness: 'When dying, they resent the loss of control over their fate and the sense of adequacy they have always striven for in life. They are angry with their own failing bodies and they are also apt to criticize and blame others.'[2]

In bereavement too, anger is a normal although sometimes frightening component. C S Lewis was angry following the death of his wife. As he looked back on disappointments, he wrote:

> What chokes every prayer and every hope is the memory of all the prayers H. and I offered and all the false hopes we had. Not hopes raised merely by our own wishful thinking; hopes encouraged, even forced upon us, by false diagnoses, by X-ray photographs, by strange remissions, by one temporary recovery that might have ranked as a miracle. Step by step we were 'led up the garden path'. Time after time, when He seemed most gracious He was really preparing the next torture.[3]

The many faces of anger

It is not always easy to recognize anger, for it wears many disguises. A husband dying of cancer becomes increasingly irritable, making excessive demands on his already worried and overworked wife. He makes her feel guilty by all his demands. Why is he so unreasonable? Because he is angry. He is angry at the prospect of death, and that anger is directed towards his wife. Elisabeth Kübler-Ross points out that anger is particularly difficult to handle because it 'is displaced in all directions and projected on to the environment at times almost at random'.[4]

Anyone can be the target for anger – doctors, nurses, hospitals, family, friends, ministers, the church, God. Colin Murray Parkes' research into bereavement revealed that, 'God and the doctors came in for a lot of angry criticism, since both were seen as having power over life and death.[5] This kind of anger should be recognized for what it is – anger related to the death of a loved one or friend. The particular individual on whom the anger is vented is almost certainly innocent and quite underserving of the hostile words heaped upon him. He is a target for that basic anger, not its cause. For anger is not always directed towards the object that gives rise to it.

Here is a widow who is very critical of her Christian friends who she feels are not doing enough for her. Time after time she slates them for not caring more for widows in the church. 'No one cares' is the frequent complaint that falls on the ears of people who have visited because they care. While there may be some justification for the criticism, more often than not, much of it is unreasonable. This bitter criticism may well be one of the masks worn by anger. The widow is angry about her whole situation, the unfairness, the loneliness, her changed status and the lack of explanations from God. This widow's anger, directed towards her friends, is nevertheless rooted in a basic non-acceptance of her situation. She is still struggling to come to terms with the unpalatable fact of being on her own.

Only God can give the humility to discern that the critical, grumbling spirit is caused not by the failings of others but by the person's own deep-seated, unresolved anger. I would venture to suggest that there is much more of this displaced anger in Christian circles than we would care to admit. We have problems with anger because we have always regarded it as a sin instead of seeing that sometimes it is normal and healthy.

It can be healthy to get angry

The complete absence of any form of anger may in fact be cause for alarm. Dr Ruth Kopp, in her book *When Someone You Love is Dying*, writes:

> Individuals who show no evidence of anger whatsoever tend to worry me. I have learned that the absence of anger often indicates either a lack of true acceptance of the fatal diagnosis on an intimately personal level, or a block within the individual between his mind and his feelings.[6]

There can be serious consequences, both physiological and psychological, from the non-expression of anger. It is dangerous to supress anger; it must have a positive outlet. Suppressed anger can lead to such diseases as ulcers, hypertension, asthma and tension headaches. Dr Rubin, in *The Angry Book*, writes of the danger of converting healthy, angry feelings into a 'slush bank'. Deep in the subconscious this 'slush' lies, throwing up any number of perversions including anxiety, disproportionate anger, depression (anger turned inwards), over-reacting, insomnia, obsessions and phobias.[7] The right expression of this natural human emotion of anger must be found, or we may become the victim of this fierce power working negatively in our bodies and minds.

Not only is it normal to get angry, we need to get angry; it is healthy; but is it Christian? Isn't anger one of the seven deadly sins? Are not 'anger' and 'wrath' among the sins that we, as Christians, are commanded to discard? Did not our Lord extend the sixth commandment, 'Do not murder', to include anger (Matt 5:22)?

It is Godlike to be angry

Anger is one of the characteristics of God. There are many references in the Bible to the anger of a holy God, an anger reflected in Jesus Christ, the image of the invisible God. When Jesus arrived in Bethany, too late to save Lazarus from dying, he sought to comfort Mary and Martha. Their anger was thinly disguised, 'Lord, if you had been here, my brother would not have died' (John 11:21,32). But they were not the only people who were angry that day. When Jesus saw the deep sorrow of Mary and the shared sorrow of her friends, he was 'deeply moved in spirit' (John 11:33). The word used here and in verse 38 to describe this deep emotion literally means to snort with anger like a horse. It is a word that indicates the divine anger of Jesus. What made Jesus so angry was the devastation caused by death. He looked on the devil's final weapon, saw its effect on people, and smouldered with anger. It is not wrong to get angry in the face of death; it is a Christlike reaction.

I recall the immense relief and witness of the Holy Spirit in my own heart on making this simple discovery. So the feelings I had in my heart about the 'violent tyranny' of death were not sinful after all. I had not been wrong to think that the death of John was a grim, ugly business. I no longer had to hide those feelings, they were all right; it was okay to feel angry about John's death. The relief was immense.

Is that how you feel about the death of someone close to you? Angry? Then stand at the graveside of Lazarus and see the Son of God shaking with divine anger at death and its cruel impact on human lives. Take heart! You are much nearer to the heart of God than you thought. You may well find that, standing right next to you, sharing your anger, feeling the injustice, and weeping with you, is Jesus Christ himself.

'Be angry and sin not'

The Bible concedes the possibility of being angry and not sinning. Quoting Psalm 4:4, 'In your anger do not sin', the apostle Paul, then spells out a practical step to take if we are to avoid anger becoming a sin: 'Do not let the sun go down while you are still angry' (Eph 4:26). Anger is energy, and as such it is morally neutral, like jealousy or ambition. 'Anger takes on a moral dimension when it is put to use.'[8]

What makes us angry and how we express that anger will determine whether or not the anger is sin. It is significant that whenever Jesus was angry he then said and did something. Just as the phrase 'moved with compassion', so often used of Jesus, is always followed by some action, so references to Jesus being angry are followed by some activity. Anger was never just a feeling Jesus experienced, it was a driving force leading to action. His anger at the graveside of Lazarus was followed by his summoning Lazarus back from the dead. Jesus was more than merely angry at death; he fought and conquered it.

So we are faced with the challenge of harnessing the energy in a constructive way, to the benefit of others as well as ourselves. To this challenge we will return later.

Coping with other people's anger

It is not easy being on the receiving end of someone else's anger. It sometimes happens that a person who is terminally ill may vent his anger on those closest to him. This 'ventilation' may take the form of sullen silences or irritability or aggressive outbursts. The expressions may vary, but the cause is the same – anger. However, the patient may be as 'nice as pie' when someone else enters the room. It is important to understand why he is so selective when it comes to expressing his anger. He will be angry with those with whom it is safe to be angry, those who will come back again, those who will continue loving in spite of everything. It is important therefore, when coping with someone else's anger, to listen. Those involved in counselling and pastoral ministries must learn to listen sympathetically, without a judgmental spirit, to people who angrily let off steam. For this 'emotional ventilation' is essential before a person can be open to counselling.[9] The dying and the bereaved should therefore be encouraged to talk about negative feelings such as anger. It is a privilege, though a very painful one, to be a 'safe' person to whom people will feel free to express their anger.

The death of a child understandably provokes deep anger. In their anger, the parents often want to blame someone; the doctor was negligent in diagnosing the problem, the surgeon did not perform the operation properly, the nurses was not attentive enough, if we hadn't gone on holiday this would never have happened, if the car had kept to the speed limit . . . and so on. Richard Lamerton, writing about these 'if only' statements, concludes, 'All this will have to be patiently listened to, like weathering a storm, because the repetition of the fears and frustrations to a listener enables them to develop insight. And this is how the process of healing begins for them.[10]

Understanding the basic cause of the anger will

enable us not to take the anger personally, although the accusations may be directed to us. We will not help the angry person if we react by being hurt or getting angry ourselves. The wife whose dying husband grumbles and criticizes her needs to know that she is not the root cause of his anger. That cause lies in the helplessness and weakness of being ill. The wife is the nearest and safest person on whom to vent this frustration.

God is a 'safe person'

There are times when our anger is directed towards God. Why does he say, 'Ask and it shall be given you', and refuse our request? We did all that it says in James 5:14,15, but the sick man died and was not 'raised up'.

With anger and in bewilderment we try to reconcile certain promises of God with our experience.

Six weeks before John died I spoke to him on the telephone. He was elated and full of hope. The consultant had examined John that day and confirmed an improvement in the condition of his liver; John was feeling stronger, had driven the car and had done some gardening. The consultant said that he was always self-critical about his diagnoses and then continued, 'I may have been wrong with the diagnosis, but I don't think so. I have either been wrong, or there has been a reversal by our Maker.' You can imagine the excitement following that phone call. Was God healing? It looked like it! In a prayer meeting the following day, we rejoiced at what God seemed to be doing. Six weeks later John died. The consultant had been wrong. Dear God, why did you let our hopes rise?

Crying out in despair and anger to God is what many of his people have done in the past. In his distress, following the devastating loss of his possessions, family and health, Job cried angrily to God, cursing the day he was born (Job 3:1–26). God in his infinite love and patience listened to the groans of Job, and understood. Like the psalmist, Job discovered that he could express his anger towards God to God himself. With no small understatement, Ruth Kopp urges us to share our anger with God: 'God is capable of handling our anger and answering our accusations.'[11] So we need not try to protect God from either our anger or from that of someone else. Archbishop Leighton of Glasgow wrote to a depressed woman in the seventeenth century, 'I bid you, vent your rage into the bosom of God.'

Only after Job had ranted and raved at God was he able to listen and to receive the revelation of God's character and power given in Job 38–41. Don't be afraid to tell God how angry you feel at your situation, whether you are facing serious illness or bereavement. Tell him how the injustice of it all hurts you. Share your disappointments with him or with a mature friend who can take you and your anger to God. It is far better to shout at God or at a wise Christian friend than to explode in anger at a committee meeting or to a person young in the faith. Our anger will not hurt God but it could hurt other people.

Do something constructive with anger

We have already noted that anger is energy and that Jesus directed this energy along positive channels. Angry at the death of Lazarus, he raised Lazarus. How can we ensure that our anger does not become sin?

We can talk to a Christian friend who will listen patiently without condemning us. We may have a lot of talking to do before all the anger is released. One conversation will rarely unlock it all.

Some find it helpful to write down their feelings. C S Lewis certainly worked through much of his anger by writing his book *A Grief Observed*. For me writing this book has been a constructive way of working through some of the painful and angry thoughts associated with John's death.

The political reformer, John Bright, learnt how to direct anger down positive channels. After the death of Bright's young wife, his friend, Richard Cobden, called to offer comfort. In the course of conversation Cobden challenged the numb and silent Bright. 'There are thousands of houses in England at this moment where wives and children are dying of hunger – hunger made by the Laws. When the first paroxysm of your grief is passed, come with me, and we will never rest until those Laws are repealed.'[12] So John Bright found in the crucible of grief the energy to campaign on behalf of the poor. Anger that could have destroyed him was channelled into an area where it was right to be angry. Anger is a fact of life, and a normal, healthy component of dying and grief. It is an emotion created by God, experienced by God and used by God. It is possible to be angry and not sin. The challenge before us is to direct the energy of anger towards constructive ends.

13
The courage to hope

My Lord God, give me once more the courage to hope
(Søren Kierkegaard)

We have been considering the needs of the dying and the families who care for them, the families who must later walk the long road of bereavement. At all stages of dying and bereavement, the constant need is for hope, not false hope that mocks, but real hope that holds us in the storm. The writer to the Hebrews saw the Christian hope as just such an anchor: 'We have this hope as an anchor for the soul, firm and secure' (Heb 6:19).

In popular usage, the word 'hope' expresses uncertainty or, at best, a vague optimism: 'He is very forgetful; I hope he comes.' What we are saying here is that there is some doubt about whether he will come; he may, he may not. The New Testament entertains no such uncertainty when it uses the word 'hope'.

Peter writes of the living hope every Christian possesses. He emphasizes the certainty of this hope when he describes the Christian's inheritance as something that 'can never perish, spoil or fade' and is 'kept in heaven for you' (1 Pet 1:4 GNB). We are told that this inheritance is given to us 'through the resurrection of Jesus Christ from the dead' (1 Pet 1:3, GNB). Furthermore, Peter explains that not only is our inheritance kept for us, but we are being kept for the inheritance through being 'shielded by God's power' (1 Pet 1:5, GNB).

The believer's inheritance is so sure that no doubt

is entertained about either the inheritance itself or the Christian's obtaining it.

Hope grounded on truth

The faith of the dying and the grieving needs to be upheld by such real hope, hope that is based on the great truths of the Christian faith. These biblical truths, learnt in the light, must then be reaffirmed amidst the darkness surrounding death. As we believe in these truths, we shall receive from God the courage to hope.

God is sovereign

We believe that God is in control of this world and of our individual lives. With Paul, we affirm that – in spite of appearances and feelings – 'in all things God works for the good of those who love him' (Rom 8:28). The hounds of heaven, goodness and love, will follow us all the days of our lives, until we 'dwell in the house of the Lord for ever' (Ps 23:6).

The tomb was empty

On the first Easter Sunday only the grave clothes lay in the Jerusalem tomb where the dead body of Jesus had been laid. Jesus Christ had risen from the dead. Death, man's greatest enemy, had been defeated and stripped of its power. As believers in Jesus Christ we share in this conquest of death. That is why at the funeral service of a believer an Easter refrain can be heard breaking through the sadness. At John's funeral the triumphant theme of the service was found in Jesus' words: 'Because I live, you also will live' (John 14:19). That same note of victory was expressed in the hymn 'Thine be the glory, risen, conquering Son . . .'

Heaven is home

Jesus said that he was going to prepare a place for his friends. God's Son, who had come from heaven, knew what he was talking about. He made no attempt to describe the 'furniture' of heaven. He was content to leave one major hope with his friends – that to be in heaven was to be at home with Jesus (John 14:1–3). Implicit within Jesus' promise is the joyful reunion with all our loved ones who are also with the Lord.

Jesus is alive

We have a travelling companion along the dark valley of death and the long road of bereavement. The psalmist was confident that no harm could come to him as he walked through the 'darkest valley' because the divine Shepherd would be with him (Ps 23:4). God, who sent his Son to be the Good Shepherd, has promised, 'Never will I leave you; never will I forsake you' (Heb 13:5).

Grace to cope

We believe that whether in dying or in grieving God's grace will always be sufficient, so that, come what may, we will be able to cope. The greater our need, the greater the possibility of discovering God, for in his love he does not waste any of our experiences of suffering but 'uses the losses of our lives and of our deaths to give us himself' (Dame Cicely Saunders).

After crossing the Red Sea, the Israelites found themselves in the desert. They grumbled, wondering where on earth they were going to find bread in a desert. They found bread on earth which had come down from heaven. At the start of every day God faithfully sent his bread (manna) to his people. In death and bereavement, God's 'manna' will be provided.

Faith sharper

After learning that he was dying of cancer, James Casson experienced an amazing and paradoxical sense of vitality: 'I suddenly became free, free to live as a person in my own right.'[1] Dying makes living real. The dying person often experiences a sharpening of focus: priorities are re-examined, secondary issues are discarded, material things are devalued as they are seen to be the more accoutrements of life. The Chinese proverb, 'There are no pockets in a shroud,' becomes startlingly relevant.

During the last months of his life John was given a new Good News Bible. There was little time left for him to use the new Bible. However, one chapter contains some underlined verses which give a clear indication of what God was saying to him. The focus of his faith was being sharpened. The underlined verses appear in Ephesians 5:

Faith giving: 'Your life must be controlled by love' (v 2);
Faith shining: 'So you must live like people who belong to the light' (v 8);
Faith searching: 'Don't be fools, then, but try to find out what the Lord wants you to do' (v 17);
Faith praising: 'In the name of our Lord Jesus Christ, always give thanks for everything to God the Father' (v 20).

As he pondered these scriptures, John's faith became sharper, focusing on the issues of life that really mattered.

Heaven nearer

God prepares his children for their departure to heaven.

The apostle Paul found that as his physical strength declined, so his spiritual strength increased. The decaying of the mortal body was accompanied by a renewing within the spirit: 'Though outwardly we are wasting away, yet inwardly we are being renewed day by day' (2 Cor 4:16). With the decline of the physical life and the strengthening of the spiritual life there comes a concentration on the life to come and a letting go of the present life: 'So we fix our eyes not on what is seen, but on what is unseen. For what is seen is temporary, but what is unseen is eternal' (2 Cor 4:18).

Giving them the courage to hope, God often brings his children to the place where they are willing to leave this life and depart for the next. David Watson commented to a friend some months before his death: 'I feel I have one foot in heaven and one on earth, and I am happy to land on either foot.'[2]

James Casson discovered that he could only overcome the disappointment of not being healed by having a clear vision of eternity. With such a vision he then saw his death as 'a short-cut to the summit' and himself as specially chosen for that route.[3]

Heaven clearer

I recall visiting an elderly couple who had been faithful workers in the first church of which I was pastor. Since I had not seen them for some time, I immediately noticed the change in them. They looked older and more infirm. The wife was ill, having only a few months to live. In the course of conversation we alighted on their favourite subject, heaven. In the past, as a young minister fresh from college, I was often floored by their knowledge and interpretation of the book of Revelation. They loved to talk about the detailed events of the last days and the significance of numbers and colours. I would listen, mesmerized and a trifle irritated.

On this day of renewed friendship the subject was the same, but the emphasis was different. They no longer wanted to debate the details of interpretation but were eager to talk about Christ's victory over death and the believer's hope of meeting him face to face. Doctrine was now sustaining their hearts and lives rather than stretching their minds and imaginations. Suffering and death force us to hold to the great truths of our faith in a new way. We argue less about the truth and lean harder upon it.

Heaven bigger

The faith of the elderly couple was standing on tiptoe, peering into the new world they were approaching. God's heaven was coming into view. The world that once had been contained within neat theories was proving too big for its containers. 'No eye has seen, no ear has heard, no mind had conceived what God has prepared for those who love him' (1 Cor 2:9).

How great will be the surprise in the heavenly world!

Just think . . .
of stepping on the shore and finding it heaven,
of taking hold of a hand and finding it God's hand,
of breathing new air and finding it celestial air,
of feeling invigorated and finding it immortality,
of passing from storm and tempest and finding it unknown calm,
of waking up and finding it HOME.

In heaven our values will be so different. Some of the things we have treasured in this life will be no more than discarded toys.

Teddy Bears

When we have set this aside –
name, reputation, history –
it will not be for us to slide
into dull uniformity.

Heaven will not level down.
These things that we identify
as most emphatically our own,
have less to do with you and me

than we can here imagine.
They stand to life as a cartoon,
mere toys of personality.
We shall forget them quite as soon

as a small child who suddenly
puts away his teddy bear
and runs quite unselfconsciously
to greet his father on the stairs.

Godfrey Rush

If some of our present treasures will appear as toys later, could it also be that some of our questions, so urgent now, will be irrelevant later?

A mystery not a mistake

During the last ten months of John's life there were many times when I wondered whether God was in control. Could there possibly be a plan behind all the suffering he endured? Even now, it is painful to recall his jaundiced, emaciated body. There are still things related to John's death that are hard to reconcile with the loving purpose of a sovereign God. The Lord has seen fit to reveal some of his purposes. But John's death will be to the glory of God – somehow.

The doubts I had about God's control have receded, although mystery remains. I believe that John's death was part of God's plan. It was not a divine mistake. Sometimes that is as far as faith can go. Taking its stand on the truth of God's word, faith shouts, 'I do believe; help me overcome my unbelief!' (Mark 9:24).

The greatness of the Christian faith lies not so much in that it provides answers to all our questions about pain and suffering. Its greatness lies in the fact that it offers a life that triumphs over the need for explanation. Taking our stand on what God has revealed about himself in the Bible, we trust him as we celebrate the festival of dying or walk the road of bereavement. For within that festival, or along that road, God will meet us. He will not fail to give us the courage to hope.

A prayer:

'May the God of hope fill you with all
joy and peace as you trust in him, so
that you may overflow with hope by
the power of the Holy Spirit' (Rom 15:13).

Appendix: Useful addresses

Various organizations

Age Concern, Bernard Sunley House, 60 Pitcairn Road, Mitcham, Surrey   Tel. 01 640 5431

Over 1,300 Age Concern groups in the UK run their own local services in cooperation with other voluntary organizations.

The Association of Crossroads Care Attendant Schemes, 94 Coton Road, Rugby, Warwickshire CV21 4LN   Tel. 0788 73653

Aims to give caring relatives some time to themselves by offering help on a regular and reliable basis through the Care Attendant Schemes.

The British Association of Cancer United Patients (BACUP), 121–123 Charterhouse Street, London EC1M 6AA   Tel. 01 608 1661

BACUP provides an information service for cancer sufferers who want to know more about their illnesses. Telephone or written enquiries can be made.

The Compassionate Friends, 6 Denmark Street, Bristol 1   Tel. 0272 292778

An association of bereaved parents offering friendship and understanding to other bereaved parents.

Cruse: The National Organization for the Widowed and their Children, 126 Sheen Road, Richmond, Surrey TW9 1UR   Tel. 01 4818/9047

Offers support to widows, widowers and their families. Runs training courses for those working with the bereaved.

The Family Welfare Association, 21 Kempson Road, London SW6 4PX Tel. 01 736 2127/8

Offers support through volunteer befrienders to families facing terminal illness and bereavement. Helpful literature also available.

The Foundation for the Study of Infant Deaths, 15 Belgrave Square, London SW1 8PS Tel. 01 235 1721 or 01 235 0965

Gives personal support (using letters, telephone calls and leaflets) where there has been a cot death. The Foundation acts as a centre of information about cot deaths for parents and professionals.

Marie Curie Memorial Foundation, 28 Belgrave Square, London SW1X 8QG Tel. 01 235 3325 or 21 Rutland Street, Edinburgh EH1 2AH Tel. 031 229 8332

The Foundation provides residential nursing, home nursing plus a counselling and advisory service.

National Association for the Welfare of Children in Hospital (NAWCH), Argyle House, 29–31 Euston Road, London NW1 2SD Tel. 01 833 2041

Founded to persuade hospitals that parents have a role to play in the care of children in hospital and to persuade parents to take that role.

National Society for Cancer Relief, The Macmillan Service, 30 Dorset Square, London NW1 6QL Tel. 01 402 8125

The Society was founded in 1911 by Douglas Macmillan, its purpose being to disseminate information on the prevention and relief of cancer.

Macmillan nurses work within hospitals, Macmillan homes, hospices and in the community.

Stillbirth and Neonatal Death Society (SANDS), Argyle House, Euston Road, London NW1 2SD Tel. 01 833 2851/2

Has established a national network of parents who are willing to help others similarly bereaved. It has published several leaflets giving information for parents.

Comfort for the bereaved

Cards and leaflets providing scripture portions and prayers can be obtained from: *The Bible Society*, Stonehill Green, Wastlea, Swindon SW5 7DG or 7 Hampton Terrace, Edinburgh EH12 5XU

Christian Publicity Organization, Garcia Estate, Canterbury Road, Worthing, W. Sussex BN13 1BW

DHSS leaflets

The leaflet 'What to do after a death' can be obtained from any social security office or by writing to: (*England and Wales*) DHSS Leaflets Unit, PO Box 21, Stanmore, Middlesex HA7 1AY: (*Scotland*) Scottish Home and Health Department, St Andrews House, Edinburgh EH1 3DE

Other DHSS leaflets relating to attendance and mobility allowances, the death grant, and widow's benefit can also be obtained from social security offices, post offices, libraries or Citizens Advice Bureaux.

Notes

1 Divine healing

1 Roger F Hurding *As Trees Walking* (The Paternoster Press 1982) pp 221–23
2 Ruth L Kopp *When Someone You Love is Dying* (Lion Publishing 1986) p 50
3 Joseph Bayly *The Last Thing We Talk About* (Scripture Union 1978) pp 86, 83
4 James H Casson *Dying – The Greatest Adventure of My Life* (Christian Medical Fellowship Publications 1980) p 37

2 To tell or not to tell?

1 Richard Lamerton *Care of the Dying* (Pelican Books 1980) p 163
2 Dame Cicely Saunders 'Telling Patients' *District Nursing* September 1965
3 as above
4 Quoted in 'Telling the Truth to a Terminally Ill Patient' *Journal of Pastoral Counselling* 15/1 (1980)
5 Ruth Kopp *When Someone You Love is Dying* (Lion Publishing 1986) p 87
6 Elisabeth Kübler-Ross *On Death and Dying* (Tavistock Publications 1978) p 27
7 Shirley du Boulay *Cicely Saunders* (Hodder & Stoughton 1984) p 170
8 Quoted in Margaret Manning *The Hospice Alternative* (Souvenir Press 1984) pp 58, 59

9 Richard Lamerton *Care of the Dying* p 33
10 Dame Cicely Saunders *Care of the Dying* (Nursing Times Booklet 1976), cited in Richard Lamerton *Care of the Dying* p 33

3 'It can't be true!'

1 David Watson *Fear No Evil* (Hodder & Stoughton 1984) p 14
2 as above
3 Ruth Kopp *When Someone You Love is Dying* (Lion Publishing 1986) pp 33, 34
4 Attributed to La Rochefoucauld (1613–80)
5 Elisabeth Kübler-Ross *On Death and Dying* (Tavistock Publications 1978) p 37

4 The pain of dying

1 C S Lewis *A Grief Observed* (Faber & Faber 1966) p 15
2 Anonymous *Nursing Mirror* 9 August 1968
3 David Watson *Fear No Evil* (Hodder & Stoughton 1984) p 83
4 Rosemary and Victor Zorza *A Way to Die* (Sphere Books 1981) p 33
5 J R W Stott *The Epistles of John* Tyndale New Testament Commentaries (The Tyndale Press 1964) p 75
6 Quoted in Rosemary and Victor Zorza *A Way to Die* p 29
7 Elisabeth Kübler-Ross *On Death and Dying* (Tavistock Publications 1978) p 46
8 Tom S West 'Death, Attitudes to' in A S Duncan, G R Dunstan, R B Welbourn (eds) *Dictionary of Medical Ethics* (Darton, Longman & Todd 1981) p 124

5 The care of the dying

1 Many people who are professionally involved in caring for the dying avoid using phrases such as 'terminal care' or 'care of the dying'. Involved as they are in the care of the living, they use the phrase 'continuing care'.
2 John Hinton *Dying* (Pelican Books 1972) p 155
3 O W Holmes 'The Poet at the Breakfast Table', quoted in Michael Mitton *The Wisdom to Listen* Grove Pastoral Series, No 5 (Grove Books 1981) p 3
4 Richard Lamerton *Care of the Dying* (Pelican Books 1980) p 57
5 From an article by Walter Bottoms 'The Leaves are Falling Faster' *Baptist Times* 10 September 1981

6 Death with dignity

1 Paul Tournier *A Doctor's Casebook in the Light of the Bible* (SCM Press 1954) p 17
2 Dame Cicely Saunders, quoted in Rosemary and Victor Zorza *A Way to Die* (Sphere Books Ltd 1981) p 29
3 From an address by Dame Cicely Saunders at the Guildhall Ceremony for the Templeton Prize, quoted in St Christopher's Hospice Annual Report 1980/81 p 15
4 Dame Cicely Saunders, quoted in Margaret Manning *The Hospice Alternative* (Souvenir Press 1984) p 114
5 Shirley du Boulay *Cicely Saunders* (Hodder & Stoughton 1984) pp 227–31
6 St Christopher's Hospice Annual Report 1982/83 pp 8, 9
7 R G Twycross *The Dying Patient* (Christian Medical Fellowship Publications 1975) p 5

8 Margaret Manning *The Hospice Alternative* p 68
9 Richard Lamerton *Care of the Dying* (Pelican Books 1980) p 31
10 Rosemary and Victor Zorza *A Way to Die* pp 198, 199
11 Sandol Stoddard *The Hospice Movement* (Jonathan Cape Ltd 1979)
12 Shirley du Boulay *Cicely Saunders* p 182

7 The funeral

1 Ingrid Trobisch *Learning to Walk Alone* (Inter-Varsity Press 1985) p 22. These words were inscribed on the family tombstone over the grave where Walter Trobisch was buried.
2 Brian Hession *Alone to Pray* (Peter Davies 1961) p 80
3 Peter Cotterell *Death: Your Questions Answered* (Kingsway Publications 1983) p 64

8 The long road

1 Glenn R Mosley 'Benefits of Religion: Unity' in Dr Austin Kutscher and Lillian Kutscher (eds) *Religion and Bereavement*
2 C S Lewis *The Four Loves* (Fontana 1963) p 111
3 Colin Murray Parkes *Bereavement* (Pelican Books 1975) p 189
4 C S Lewis *A Grief Observed* (Faber & Faber 1966) p 47
5 Colin Murray Parkes *Bereavement* p 21
6 C S Lewis *A Grief Observed* p 43
7 Ingrid Trobisch *Learning to Walk Alone* (Inter-Varsity Press 1985) pp 92, 93
8 as above p 94

9 Help along the road

1 John V Taylor *The Go-Between God* (SCM Press 1972) p 243
2 Colin Murray Parkes *Bereavement* (Pelican Books 1975) p 191
3 as above p 194
4 as above p 193

10 The loss of a child

1 Joan Hagan Arnold and Penelope Buschman Gemma *A Child Dies: a portrait of family grief* (Aspen Publications 1983) p 42
2 as above p 35
3 Harriet Sarnoff Schiff *The Bereaved Parent* (Souvenir Press 1979) p 60
4 as above p 58
5 as above

11 Too young to understand?

1 Sula Wolf *Children Under Stress* (Pelican Books 1981) p 100
2 Pat Wynnejones *Children, Death and Bereavement* (Scripture Union 1985) p 95

12 Anger

1 Christine Simpson 'Nobody Told Me' *Nursing Mirror* 9 November 1983, Supplement p xi
2 John Hinton *Dying* (Pelican Books 1972) p 90
3 C S Lewis *A Grief Observed* (Faber & Faber 1966) pp 26, 27

4 Elisabeth Kübler-Ross *On Death and Dying* (Tavistock Publications 1978) p 44
5 Colin Murray Parkes *Bereavement* (Pelican Books 1975) p 103
6 Ruth Kopp *When Someone You Love is Dying* (Lion Publishing 1986) p 154
7 Dr Theodore Rubin *The Angry Book* (McMillan Collier 1969), quoted in Myra Chave-Jones *Be Angry and Sin Not* (Care and Counsel/Scripture Union 1983) p 9
8 Myra Chave-Jones *Be Angry and Sin Not* p 7
9 Howard J Clinebell Jr *Basic Types of Pastoral Counselling* (Abingdon Press 1966) p 170
10 Richard Lamerton *Care of the Dying* (Pelican Books 1980) p 112
11 Ruth Kopp *When Someone You Love is Dying* p 170
12 Quoted in William Purcell *A Time to Die* (Mowbrays 1978) p 131

13 The courage to hope

1 James H Casson *Dying – The Greatest Adventure of My Life* (Christian Medical Fellowship Publications 1980) p 19
2 Rev Teddy Saunders 'The Final Years' in Edward England (ed) *David Watson: A Portrait by His Friends* (Highland Books 1985) p 201
3 James H Casson *Dying – The Greatest Adventure of My Life* p 31

Further reading

Ruth Kopp *When Someone You Love is Dying* (Lion Publishing 1986) The care of the terminally ill is given a thorough treatment by a Christian doctor. The biblical insights and practical suggestions help both the terminally ill and those caring for them.

David Watson *Fear No Evil* (Hodder and Stoughton 1984) A book remarkable for the faith and honesty of its author who wrestles with the issues of suffering and healing while himself suffering from cancer.

Wendy Green *The Long Road Home* (Lion Publishing 1986) The mother of four children records her experience of watching her husband die and then facing life without him. A disarmingly honest, down-to-earth book.

Elizabeth Heike *A Question of Grief* (Hodder & Stoughton 1985) A well-written, sensitive account of the author's bereavement at the death of a close friend. Through the pain and bewilderment of grief, faith can grow.

Ingrid Trobisch *Learning to Walk Alone* (Inter-Varsity Press 1985) The author reflects on her grief following the death of her husband. A positive book in which honesty is tempered by sensitivity and maturity.

Pat Wynnejones *Children, Death and Bereavement* (Scripture Union 1985) This book is the product of much research into how children of different ages understand death. It contains many insights into how to talk to children about death.

Jim Graham *Dying to Live* (Marshall Morgan & Scott 1984) A biblical exposition of teaching on life after death. The hope of heaven is explored, while the darker side of death is not ignored.

Warren Wiersbe *Why Us? When Bad Things Happen to God's People* (Inter-Varsity Press 1984) A book on suffering that asks awkward questions, gives honest biblical answers and sheds some light on the subject.

Shirley du Boulay *Cicely Saunders* (Hodder & Stoughton 1984) A fascinating, well-researched biography of the pioneer of the modern hospice movement.